MATHILDE FRANZISKA ANNEKE (1817–1884)

PETER LANG
New York • Washington, D.C./Baltimore • Bern
Frankfurt am Main • Berlin • Brussels • Vienna • Oxford

SUSAN L. PIEPKE

MATHILDE FRANZISKA ANNEKE (1817–1884)

The Works and Life of a German-American Activist
including English translations of "Woman in Conflict with Society" and "Broken Chains"

PETER LANG
New York • Washington, D.C./Baltimore • Bern
Frankfurt am Main • Berlin • Brussels • Vienna • Oxford

Library of Congress Cataloging-in-Publication Data

Piepke, Susan L.
Mathilde Franziska Anneke (1817–1884): the works and life
of a German-American activist (including English translations
of Woman in conflict with society and Broken chains) / Susan L. Piepke.
p. cm.
Includes bibliographical references and index.
1. Anneke, Mathilde Franziska Giesler, 1817–1884.
2. Women social reformers—United States—Biography. 3. Suffragists—
United States—Biography. 4. German American women—Biography.
5. Women's rights. 6. Women—Education. 7. Germany—
History—Revolution, 1848–1849. I. Title.
HQ1413.A52P54   305.42'092—dc22   2005010689
ISBN 0-8204-7913-6

Bibliographic information published by **Die Deutsche Bibliothek**.
Die Deutsche Bibliothek lists this publication in the "Deutsche
Nationalbibliografie"; detailed bibliographic data is available
on the Internet at http://dnb.ddb.de/.

Cover design by Sophie Boorsch Appel

The paper in this book meets the guidelines for permanence and durability
of the Committee on Production Guidelines for Book Longevity
of the Council of Library Resources.

Table of Contents

Acknowledgments

A project like this book on the life and works of Mathilde Franziska Anneke grows out of previous projects and research and always involves a number of institutions and individuals who have been particularly helpful in its final completion. I am very grateful to all of them, and while it is not possible to mention here everyone whose encouragement along the way helped keep me focused on this work, there are certainly several who especially deserve my public thanks.

The idea for this work had its beginning during some early research on German women writers of the nineteenth century. This research was generously supported by a National Endowment for the Humanities Summer Study Grant, and I think that without this important start in looking at these materials, I never would have found the exciting materials that formed the basis for my subsequent research and writing. This particular grant provided "seed money" for professors with heavy teaching loads at small liberal-arts colleges to take time in the summer to pursue a research project. This is the second book to come from this initial project.

Bridgewater College, where I have taught since 1988, has provided strong support for my work both in grant monies and in time for developing both of my books. For the current project, a College Faculty Research Grant provided funding so that I could finish my research. In addition, a well-timed sabbatical allowed me to complete final writing on the manuscript. It was also through the support of the College administration that I received a Mednick Grant for essential research at the Historical Society of Wisconsin in Madison. I would like to add a word of gratitude to the Virginia Foundation for Independent Colleges for providing funding to faculty from the member colleges through their Mednick Grant program.

A special thanks goes to the excellent libraries and archives where I conducted my research. It is very often difficult to find and gain access to materials on nineteenth-century German women writers. The Bridgewater College library staff, who would tell me they were only doing their job, has always gone above and beyond the call of duty to help me find what I need. In addition, the helpful staff at the Sophia Smith Collection at Smith College provided me with fascinating materials regarding the Woman Suffrage Movement, which spurred this new project even while I was working on my earlier book on Luise Büchner. And certainly without the many materials in the Anneke Collection at the Wisconsin Historical Society, Madison, along with the assistance of the excellent staff, this project would not have been possible. The two photographs of Mathilde Franziska Anneke included in this book are reprinted with permission of the Wisconsin Historical Society.

A final personal thanks goes to my colleagues and friends at Bridgewater College for all their encouragement and suggestions. A belated thank you to the patient general editor of my earlier book on Luise Büchner, Peter D.G. Brown—your contribution to that project is something that I will always value. Finally, without a doubt, my greatest debt of gratitude is to my family, especially to Walter Piepke, whose love and support are absolutely essential on this and all my projects.

Susan L. Piepke

Mathilde Anneke at about 25 years old. Photograph from a drawing.
Wisconsin Historical Society WHi-7882

Formal studio portrait of Mathilde Franziska Anneke
Wisconsin Historical Society WHi-3701

Chapter 1

Introduction

The years of Mathilde Franziska Anneke's life, 1817–1884, spanned interesting historical times in Germany, where she lived the first part of her life, and in the United States, where she settled after the failure of the Revolution of 1848. Anneke participated in the heady liberal discussions of the *Vormärz*, founded a short-lived revolutionary newspaper, and even rode into battle in Germany. She actively participated in the Woman Suffrage Movement and the Anti-Slavery Movement in the United States, using her journalistic and oratory skills. She was on the forefront of some of the most exciting social changes of the nineteenth century; she was a political activist, writer, and educator—yet today her name is little known on either side of the Atlantic.

Until relatively recently, most nineteenth-century women writers had been relegated to the forgotten past. A few, Annette von Droste-Hülshoff and Marie von Ebner-Eschenbach among them, wrote literature that has been included in literary anthologies and is respected for its quality. Current research continues to explore various aspects of their work, and to include them in discussions of lesser-known writers whose work is being rediscovered. Carol Diethe's book, *Towards Emancipation: German Women Writers of the Nineteenth Century* (1998), in which she presents the life and work of twenty women writers, is a recent example of this type of important contribution to nineteenth-century research. Translations into English, such as Helga H. Harriman's *Seven Stories by Marie von Ebner-Eschenbach*, or the anthology of eighteenth- and nineteenth-century fiction edited by Jeannine Blackwell and Susanne Zantop entitled *Bitter Healing: German Women Writers from 1700–1830*, make some of their work accessible to those who do not read German. Other women authors, whose work was dismissed as imitative and uninteresting, are being rediscovered for the passion of their essays and the social force of their fiction. Since many of these texts are not easily accessible, those that have been reissued in modern form are particularly valuable. Renate Möhrmann's *Frauenemanzipation im deutschen Vormärz: Texte und Dokumente* (1978), for example, includes excerpts from works by Fanny Lewald, Malvida von Meysenbug, Louise Otto-Peters, Luise Dittmar, Ida Hahn-Hahn, Luise Mühlbach, Louise Aston, and Mathilde Franziska Anneke. Two examples in English are Fanny Lewald's *Meine Lebensgeschichte* (translated as: *The Education of Fanny Lewald: An Autobiography*. Hanna Ballin Lewis, Albany: SUNY Press, 1992) and Luise Büchner's 1855 essay, *Die Frauen und ihr Beruf* (available as *Women and Their Vocation: A Nineteenth-Century View by Luise Büchner*, New York: Peter Lang, 1999), in which she argues strongly for the reform of women's education. Because of her life as an activist whose views are reflected in her essays and fiction, Mathilde Franziska Anneke should, in my view, also be included in the category of women writers who merit greater attention in nineteenth-century research.

The writings of nineteenth-century women writers covered the full range of issues important to women, generally using formats acceptable for women, including letters, travelogues, biography, poetry, and novels. In the early nineteenth century, letters were a major form of self-expression for women. As Margaretmary Daley shows in her book, *Women of Letters: A Study of Self and Genre in the Personal Writing of Caroline Schlegel-Schelling, Rahel Levin Varnhagen, and Bettina von Arnim* (1998), a book composed of literary letters allowed talented women writers to use this genre "to explore the complexities and nuances of female self-definition" (ix). The letters chronicled the events and culture around the writer and gave accounts of famous people they met in the literary salons of the time. However, as Daley demonstrates, the writers' principal interest was a voyage of self-discovery, an "unfolding of their private lives" (ix), and she also provides translations of selected letters. The publication of Varnhagen's letters in *Rahel: Ein Buch des Andenkens für ihre Freunde* (*Rahel: A Book of Remembrance for Her Friends*) in 1834 had a tremendous influence on many nineteenth-century women writers. In her chapter in the 1989 study *Out of Line/Ausgefallen: The Paradox of Marginality in the Writings of Nineteenth-Century German Women* (Joeres & Burkhard 95–113), Edith Waldstein notes Varnhagen's role in bringing together aspiring intellectuals at the turn of the century. In *Towards Emancipation*, Diethe captures the paradox of this influential woman's life when she writes: "in spite of the fact that her contemporaries chose to see her position as becomingly feminine, Rahel Varnhagen has served as an inspiration for generations of women writers of more radical stamp" (31), including Fanny Lewald (1811–1889), Malvida von Meysenbug (1816–1903), and Hedwig Dohm (1831–1913). Even the more conservative writer and educational reformer, Luise Büchner, was influenced by Varnhagen's work, as evidenced by her use of quotes from her letters (Büchner identifies her as Rahel) as mottos for some of the chapters (see chapters 5 and 13) in her major work, *Die Frauen und ihr Beruf*. Lorely French looks at letters as an outlet for women's creativity in her 1996 book, *German Women as Letter Writers: 1750–1850*, and notes that feminist scholarship has taken new interest in the study of genres outside of the canon, which women used to explore their personal experience. Letters remain important to researchers looking at the life and thoughts of Mathilde Anneke as well, although hers are not literary as were those of the writers mentioned above. Anneke developed into a political being through her personal experience and the atmosphere of revolution in the period around 1848. Her early life did not seem to foreshadow her intense, lifelong involvement in political movements, but her contact with a circle of intellectuals and political activists stimulated her to develop her own thoughts concerning constitutional politics and women's emancipation. Her writing took place in a more public forum, and her means of self-actualization was not through letters in which private experiences were subjectively examined. However, she did leave a collection of letters, which allows the modern researcher to gather data about her life, especially about her life after her marriage to Fritz Anneke.

Travelogues are an excellent source of writings by women seeking to describe and understand other cultures, and thereby also understand themselves and their own culture. The role of woman as "other" is the basis of *Encountering the Other(s): Studies in Literature, History, and Culture*, edited by Gisela Brinker-Gabler (1995), and Stephanie Ohnesorg explores the role of travelogues by women writers in *Mit Kompaß, Kutsche und Kamel* (1996; *With Compass, Carriage, and Camel*). Writers like Ida Hahn-Hahn sought out exotic cultures, which she described in *Orientalische Briefe* (1844). Others, like Luise Büchner and Fanny Lewald, traveled closer to home, writing about Germany and neighboring European countries. Travelogues were often written by women as "bread and butter" work, meant to provide for their livelihood, as may well have been the case for Mathilde Franziska's *Eine*

Reise im Mai 1843 (Ruben 12), but they also could be used to reveal a political point of view or to explore a deeper question. Luise Büchner, for example, used her essay "Eine Reise-Erinnerung" (1875; "A Travel Memoire"), to praise the Swiss university system for admitting women to study medicine on an equal basis with men, and to explore the difficulties of balancing a professional career with raising a family (Büchner, *Women and Their Vocation*, Introduction, 16–17).

It is perhaps her political activism that most defines Mathilde Franziska Anneke, and that is reflected in her writings and her life work. She participated fully and significantly in the major political movements of her time. Although born in Germany, Anneke led a life with many parallels to the lives of the well-known women who would later drive the Woman Suffrage Movement. She was born two years after Elizabeth Cady Stanton and was the contemporary of major figures in the movement such as Susan B. Anthony, and Ernestine L. Rose, who emigrated from Poland and served as Anneke's interpreter on several occasions. Her views on women's rights were as radical as those of Anthony and Stanton, and her commitment to Woman Suffrage was a driving force in her life almost from the moment of her arrival in the United States.

Political rights were restricted in Anneke's homeland, but not only for women. The written word, in pamphlets and newspapers, helped raise public consciousness and argued for political change. The nineteenth century in the United States was a time of restricted political rights, specifically voting rights, followed by intense political activism to obtain those rights. Most state constitutions did not allow women to vote, and the United States Constitution made no specific references to women in regard to the franchise. That would change with the Fourteenth Amendment.[1] Interestingly, New Jersey residents, both men and women ("worth 50 pounds proclamation money") could vote during the period 1783–1807, after which time that right was restricted to white males of property. This change in voting practice was said to be "highly necessary to the safety, quiet, good order and dignity of the state" and applied to aliens, women, and persons of color (Frost & Cullen-DuPont 13).

Education for women became an issue in the nineteenth century both in Germany and in the United States. The much-repeated question, "What do women want?" was a major area of discussion in the press and in the church. Psychologists such as Freud sought scientific answers. Prominent church officials supported the tradition of keeping women in the home, isolated from

the public sphere, as an important aspect of an idealized domesticity. However, during this period, even women who accepted the idea of a separate
sphere for women became acutely aware of the need for better education.
The arguments from their side often focused on the need for education so
that women could be better educators of their children, more effective within
their domestic sphere, and more interesting companions and full partners for
their husbands.[2] Education was often valued for its own sake rather than as
job training, although pragmatic arguments were regularly mentioned. These
arguments were not initially directed toward the idea of women earning their
own living—at least not for married woman of the upper and middle classes,
where a working wife or daughter might reflect negatively on the father of
the family. Fanny Lewald discusses German attitudes in this regard in her
autobiography; John L. Rury describes the situation in the United States in
his study, *Education and Women's Work*. Looking at the later part of the
century and the early twentieth century (1870–1930), Rury points out, too,
that the issue of education and work for women was "marked by a curious
dialectic of opportunity and constraint" (3). Indeed, he states explicitly,
"Widening receptivity to women in education, it seems, was not always accompanied by growing opportunities in women's work. And when female
work roles changed most dramatically, opening new areas of employment,
women's education appears to have become more restrictive" (3).

In both Germany and the United States, a distinction was made regarding
the freedom offered to single women as opposed to married women. The
married woman paid for her new status in society by becoming a *femme cou-*
verte (Frost & Cullen-DuPont 1) under common law and being subject to her
husband who was to protect her. When in marriage the man and wife became
one, that "one" was clearly the husband, who retained all of his rights as he
gained control over his wife's person and property (Frost & Cullen-DuPont
2). Alexis de Tocqueville's observations of American women in 1831–32 in
Democracy in America are particularly telling: "In America the independence of women is irrecoverably lost in the bonds of matrimony: if an unmarried woman is less constrained there than elsewhere, a wife is subjected to
stricter obligations. The former makes her father's house an abode of freedom and of pleasure; the latter lives in the home of her husband as if it were
a cloister.... Religious peoples and trading nations entertain peculiarly serious notions of marriage: the former consider the regularity of woman's life
as the best pledge and most certain sign of the purity of her morals; the latter
regard it as the highest security for the order and prosperity of the household.

The Americans are at the same time a puritanical people and a commercial nation: their religious opinions, as well as their trading habits, consequently lead them to require much abnegation on the part of woman, and a constant sacrifice of her pleasures to her duties which is seldom demanded of her in Europe. Thus in the United States the inexorable opinion of the public carefully circumscribes woman within the narrow circle of domestic interests and duties, and forbids her to step beyond it" (Cited from Frost & Cullen-DuPont 19–20).

This, then, is the atmosphere of nineteenth-century America into which Anneke and her husband brought their liberal ideas from the Revolution of 1848 in Germany.

Mathilde Franziska Anneke left an extensive body of work, including essays, poetry, novels, short stories, a play, translations, and countless newspaper articles and editorials, as well as a collection of personal letters. In addition, she delivered many speeches in favor of the cause of Woman Suffrage in America, and some of that material is available in the Anneke Collection of the Wisconsin Historical Society in Madison. There are several sources of information on Anneke's life and work, but the most important research has been done by Maria Wagner and is available in her 1980 book, *Mathilde Franziska Anneke in Selbstzeugnissen und Dokumenten*, and her articles, including "A German Writer and Feminist in 19th-Century America," which appears in *Beyond the Eternal Feminine: Critical Essays on Women and German Literature* (1982). I will discuss Anneke's major works in the context of her life and have included a translation of the full text of her important essay in defense of Louise Aston, "Das Weib im Conflict mit den socialen Verhaeltnissen" ("Woman in Conflict with Society"), and her short story demonstrating in emotional terms the human cost of slavery, "Die Gebrochenen Ketten" ("Broken Chains").

In her own time, Anneke was well known for her writing, both journalistic and fictional, and for her social activism. An unpublished typed manuscript written by Hertha Anneke Sanne and Henrietta M. Heinzen for the National League of Women Voters for their Honor Roll in Washington, DC, can be found in the Anneke Collection of the Wisconsin Historical Society in Madison. The tone and the writers' point of view regarding the significance of Anneke's life for women of the nineteenth and early twentieth centuries, as well as the condensed overview of her many contributions, combine to make a fitting introduction to this book on her life and work:[3]

Mathilde Franziska Anneke: Poet, Journalist, Orator, Educator, Libertarian

The life of Mathilde Franziska Anneke, leader in the movement for the advancement of women, belongs in the nineteenth century, but the influence of her ideas and inspiring endeavors extends into the present time, in which many of her radical and democratic ideals have been realized by means of legislation.

According to an able student of the German element in the United States, Dr. A.B. Faust of Cornell University, Mathilde Franziska Anneke was undoubtedly the most heroic figure among the many noble types of German women who have come to this country. A talented poet and dramatist, a founder of radical journals, a devoted wife and mother, she was above all others the champion of human liberty, social, political and intellectual, and was surpassed by neither man nor woman of her generation in her ardent and fearless advocacy of freedom and justice.

Mathilde Franziska Giesler was born on her grandfather's estate, near Blankenstein, Westphalia, on April 3, 1817. Her father was Karl Giesler, King's Counsellor, a godchild of the great statesman, Baron von Stein. The beauty of her surroundings, both here and at the castle of Blankenstein where she grew up, made an indelible impression on her sensitive imagination and helped to shape her poetic genius.

In her nineteenth year she married a Westphalian nobleman, Alfred von Tabouillot, and from this time on her life took on a more sombre aspect. The marriage proved very unhappy, and after a year she was granted a divorce. By her eloquent plea she succeeded in keeping the custody of her infant daughter. She became widely known during her divorce proceedings by means of articles in the *Kölnische Zeitung,* which aroused the sympathy of the public. It was at this time, 1837, that she became conscious of the degrading social status of women, and began to work for their enfranchisement. She was the first public advocate of women's rights in Germany, with a gift of oratory seldom surpassed. Her book *Woman in Conflict with Social Conditions* won for her a national reputation, and resulted in changes in the laws relating to marriage and divorce.

Thus her home in Köln became the meeting place of many of Germany's greatest men of letters and radical leaders. Among these she met Fritz Anneke, a Prussian officer who had been forced to resign because of radical activities. He was attracted by her beauty and charm as well as by her ardor for freedom. They married in 1847 and joined the German revolutionists in their struggle for constitutional rights. Anneke became a powerful leader and when he was imprisoned because of his incendiary articles, she continued the publication of his journal, the *Neue Kolnische Zeitung*, in her own home. The paper was suppressed, but she then started publication of the *Frauen Zeitung* (*Women's Journal*), the first woman's rights periodical.

Upon his acquittal Anneke joined the People's Party as Commander of Artillery in the Palatinate. At his urgent pleas his wife followed him into the field and served as his mounted orderly, together with Carl Schurz, who in his Memoirs describes her as "a young woman of noble character, beauty, vivacity and fiery patriotism." She did duty now in the thickest of the fray, now carrying comfort or help to the wounded, and at the close of each day she slept as soldiers sleep on the battlefield, at the feet of her faithful horse. One of her countrymen says, "Through all this time she was never a burden, she never needed protection for herself and her perfect womanliness never failed."

After futile battles and defeat, the republican armies surrendered and the leaders were sentenced to death. Fritz Anneke and his wife fled to Switzerland, thence through France to America, where they landed toward the end of 1849.

They settled in Milwaukee, and Madam Anneke soon became a speaker before large audiences and toured the country giving addresses on literary subjects, on the recent revolutionary activities, and on the emancipation of women. In 1852 she again published her paper, the *Frauen Zeitung*.[4]

Madam Anneke was probably the most noted speaker in her native tongue in America. Her eloquence was compared by Grace Greenwood to that of Kossuth, the great Hungarian. In the course of her work she naturally met and became the friend of the foremost American suffrage leaders, and particularly of Susan B. Anthony and Elizabeth Cady Stanton. Her personal correspondence gives evidence of the respect and affection these women felt for her. At the International Council of Women in Berlin, many years later, Susan B. Anthony testified to the fact that her first stand for woman suffrage was due to the inspiration of Madam Anneke, who in the earlier decades had braved with her the violence of popular prejudice.

Madam Anneke addressed suffrage meetings in many eastern cities in those early days. The first suffrage convention she attended was in 1852 [sic],[5] at the Broadway Tabernacle in New York, where the delegates were attacked by mobs. In the midst of her speech (which was translated by

Ernestine Rose), she was interrupted, and the tumult was quieted only by the heroic appeal of Wendell Phillips. When she could finally be heard, she said in part: "Before I came here, I knew the tyranny and oppression of kings.... Here at least, we ought to be able to express our opinions on all subjects; and yet it would appear there is no freedom even here to claim human rights, although the only hope in (Germany)...for freedom of speech and action is directed to this country for illustration and example. That freedom I claim..." At this convention she was made vice-president. Twenty-five years later she spoke in the same place and contrasted her reception on the two occasions.

In 1860 she went to Switzerland as a newspaper correspondent with her children and her friend, the American poet, Mary Booth, and remained five years. After the Civil War, in which her husband had taken an active part, she returned and opened a school for young girls in Milwaukee. To this school she devoted the remainder of her life. Her remarkable influence as a teacher was due to her unusual personality and sympathetic understanding, as much as to her scholarship and talents, and is finely expressed by one of her former students, as follows:

"Those who have not known this great-souled woman in her activities as educator...have not seen her most beautiful traits. All who had the joy of calling her Teacher have such reverence for her that they consider her the greatest factor in their lives. It was not only what she taught but how she taught. The driest subject became a live interest. She could kindle enthusiasm with irresistible power; yet the knowledge we gained was the least of what we took away from her. Our whole beings were permeated with all that was noble and pure. She gave us the indelible stamp of her beautiful spirit. To follow her we had to aim at the stars. Never can we thank her enough for the way of feeling and thinking that she impressed upon us.

Today, pupils of Madam Anneke are unmistakable. Whether surrounded by luxuries, or confronted by the misfortunes and poverty of an adverse world, the undaunted spirit that she instilled is paramount. We try to bestow the teachings of our beloved priestess upon our children. Her only living daughter carries her exalted, beautiful message into wider circles...and so the spirit of this great woman still flames in our generation to enrich and dignify life."

Never a woman of means, she continued to devote time and strength as far as possible to the cause of women, regardless of derision and material sacrifice. Her last years were filled with illness and suffering, but her spirit continued unsubdued. She carried on her school almost to the end, and at her death (November 25, 1884) she left for her co-workers in the woman's movement words of encouragement and cheer. Firm in her principles, she never throughout life considered self, but served unceasingly the cause of freedom which was so near to her heart. [6]

Notes

1. See Frost and Cullen-DuPont, 169ff, for a discussion of this amendment and its impact on the Woman Suffrage Movement.

2. See Luise Büchner, *Women and Their Vocation: A Nineteenth-Century View* (New York: Peter Lang, 1999) for an example of the arguments used by more conservative women's rights advocates.

3. The text from here to the end of the chapter is the full Sanne/Heinzen typed text from the Wisconsin Historical Society archives. Endnotes 4 and 5 are my explanations. Note 6 indicates the sources they mention in a note at the end of their typed manuscript.

4. In March 1852 Anneke issued her newspaper under the full title, *Deutsche Frauen-Zeitung*, founding the first feminist newspaper published by a woman in the United States.

5. Although the Sanne/Heinzen typed text gives the year as 1852, the "Mob Convention," as it has been called, in New York City where Anneke spoke was September 6 and 7, 1853, according to Volume 1 of *The History of Woman Suffrage*. This is also the date cited by M. Wagner in *Mathilde Franziska Anneke in Selbstzeugnissen und Dokumenten*.

6. Sources cited by authors Hertha Anneke Sanne and Henriette M. Heinzen include Elizabeth Cady Stanton, Susan B. Anthony, and Matilda Joslyn Gage, *The History of Woman Suffrage*, 4 vols.; Wilhelm Hense-Jensen and Ernst Bruncken, *Wisconsins Deutsch-Amerikaner*, Milwaukee, 1900–1902; Regina Ruben, *Mathilde Franziska Anneke*, Hamburg; A.B. Faust, *Memoirs of Mathilde Franziska Geisler-Anneke*, German-American Annals, University of Pennsylvania, May–August 1918; Newspaper articles and other information in the possession of Mrs. Hertha Anneke Sanne, Alhambra, California.

Chapter 2

Formation of a Political Activist in the Period of German Revolution

From the collection of letters and manuscripts at the Wisconsin Historical Society in Madison, and from Maria Wagner's book *Mathilde Franziska Anneke in Selbstzeugnissen und Dokumenten* (1980), can be gleaned some basic information about Mathilde Franziska Anneke's life before her marriage to Fritz Anneke and the revolutionary period of 1848. Understandably, the focus of most of the research on Mathilde Anneke has been her activities during the period of the Revolution of 1848 and afterwards.

She was born on April 3, 1817, in Lerchenhausen (also referred to as Leveringhausen), Westphalia, on her grandfather's estate. Her parents were Karl Giesler, a wealthy mine owner, who held the position of king's counsellor (*Domänenrat*), and Elizabeth Hülswitt. Her mother did not have much formal education, but Mathilde admired her greatly and considered her an inspiration throughout her life.

In 1820 the family moved to the castle of Blankenstein in the Ruhr area. Mathilde Franziska was the oldest of twelve children and received a reasonably good education for her time. Like other German women writers of the nineteenth century, she did not attend school, but had a tutor at home and was stimulated to read widely by the number of learned people who visited her family. Fanny Lewald (see: *The Education of Fanny Lewald: An Autobiography*) and Luise Büchner (see: the introduction to *Women and Their Vocation: A Nineteenth-Century View*) were also educated in a similar manner, as was customary among the educated middle and upper classes. Mathilde Franziska had both a vivid imagination and an excellent memory; her appreciation of the value of education was evidenced throughout her life, but most especially when she founded her school in Milwaukee in her later years. There she applied the principles that she found essential for a good education to the education of young women, whom she felt were often given an education inferior to that of young men. Both Fanny Lewald and Luise Büchner wrote eloquently on the subject, as did such writers as Malvida von Meysenbug and Louise Otto-Peters (see excerpts in Möhrmann *Frauenemanzipation im deutschen Vormärz*, for example). Anneke's interest in female education places her clearly among this group of reformers.

From Blankenstein, the family moved to the small town of Haltingen (1834) where her father's speculation caused financial difficulties. Her father died on June 26, 1847, and his widow received guardianship of the five minor children: Julius Ignatz (b. 1826), Elizabeth Pauline (b. 1828), Fredericke Maria (b. 1831), Johanna Elizabeth (b. 1833), and Maria Elizabeth (b. 1848). Mathilde Franziska was close to her family throughout her life. In 1849, when Mathilde Franziska and Fritz Anneke went to America, her brothers Karl (second in age to Mathilde) and Julius were already there; later her mother and daughters Maria and Johanna settled in Milwaukee where Mathilde lived.

In 1836, at the age of 19, Mathilde Franziska married Alfred von Tabouillot, a wealthy wine merchant from Mühlheim. Her daughter Fanny was born November 28, 1837. The marriage was a very unhappy one, and the couple separated after only a year and a half. Their divorce became legal in 1843. After leaving her marriage, Mathilde Franziska moved to Münster where she and her daughter suffered financially in very difficult times. Mathilde Franziska used her writing as a journalist to support them. During this period she also wrote two prayer books (which initially had the approval of the Bishop of Münster), translated material from English and French, and was editor for two *Almanachs*, as well as a *Westfälisches Jahrbuch* (*Yearbook from Westphalia*), which included writing by Ferdinand Freiligrath and Annette von Droste-Hülshoff (Wagner, *MFA in Selbstzeugnissen* 9–10). Her drama *Oithono, oder die Tempelweihe* (*Oithono, or the Consecration of the Temple*) appeared in 1844 and was presented on the stage of Lippe-Detmold.

The position in society of a divorced woman was a difficult one. Society's attitude is reflected in a letter written by Annette von Droste-Hülshoff in which she notes her mother's desire to avoid Mathilde Franziska, and Droste-Hülshoff herself approves of that opinion (Wagner, *MFA in Selbstzeugnissen* 28–29). A divorced woman, even an innocent one, was spurned in society as "*genant*,"[1] which could be translated as "infamous," or "the subject of gossip." Reports in the liberal press of the *Vormärz* period were more sympathetic, but "decent society" (*die gute Gesellschaft*) was unable to accept a woman who sued for divorce, even when the husband was abusive, as seems to have been the case here. Furthermore, the judicial system made clear the inferior legal position of women. As Mathilde Franziska writes: "Nach dem Ausgang eines unglücklichen Scheidungsprozesses meiner ersten Ehe, worin ich ein Opfer der preußischen Justiz wurde, war ich zum Bewußtsein gekommen und zur Erkenntnis, daß die Lage der Frauen eine absurde und der Entwürdigung der Menschheit gleich bedeutende sei, begann ich früh durch Wort und Schrift für die geistige und sittliche Erhebung des Weibes so viel ich vermochte zu wirken" (quoted from Henkel 11). (After the results of an unfortunate divorce proceeding in regard to my first marriage, in which I became the victim of Prussian justice, I became conscious of the fact that the position of women is an absurd and humanly degrading one [and] I began early on through writing and speaking to take action as much as I was able for the intellectual and societal advancement of women.)

She had to fight long and hard to retain custody of her daughter, and although she won her case in court for *Unterhaltsbeihilfe* (monetary support), the sum granted was extremely small, a mere 8 Taler per month, which Henkel compares to the sum of 700 Taler that Karl Marx spent during two semesters as a student! (12).

Her experience with the legal system, and her difficulties in earning a living for herself and her daughter, clearly radicalized her thinking and made her aware of the inequities facing women in her society. Also during that time (1846), Mathilde Franziska had access to Theodor Gottlieb von Hippel's book *Über die bürgerliche Verbesserung der Weiber* (*On the Civil Improvement of Women*), written in 1792, in which he argued that women have a right to educational and employment opportunities outside of the domestic sphere, and that without such opportunities, women could not become full contributing members of society. He recognized no innate female inferiority and concluded that women's exclusion from the public sphere could be attributed to historical reasons alone, although he, like other writers into the nineteenth century, believed that men and women were of different natures. This book had tremendous influence on educated women in Germany and beyond. Even the more conservative Luise Büchner refers briefly to Hippel's work in her essay *Über weibliche Berufsarten* (7), and the context makes clear that she expected her readers to be familiar with his ideas. Many would date the debate on women's sphere from the appearance of this pivotal work (Evans 14). Indeed, the nineteenth-century social movements, including the women's movement, grew out of eighteenth-century Enlightenment ideas of the individual as a rational being, who should be able to break with the strict hierarchy of society in order to participate in self-determination (Frevert 11).

Mathilde Franziska Anneke's later work for women's enfranchisement in the United States, as well as her immediate advocacy of women's rights in Germany was, however, first and foremost a result of personal experience. Her work "Das Weib im Conflict mit socialen Verhaeltnissen" ("Woman in Conflict with Society") demonstrates her eloquence on issues relating to women's social status, particularly relating to the laws on marriage and divorce.

Mathilde Franziska became widely known during the legal proceeding surrounding her divorce because of articles that appeared in the *Kölnische Zeitung* (*Cologne Newspaper*). In Münster, she had her first contact with the democratic movement, and both in Münster and later in Cologne, she was part of a *Demokratischer Verein*, a group of young intellectuals and radical leaders. Discussions in this group ranged from music, art, and literature to political and social problems. Her liberal ideas, as well as her association with this group, must have made Mathilde Franziska all the more unacceptable to conservative society, including Droste-Hülshoff. It was within this group that she met Fritz Anneke, a Prussian officer who was discharged for liberal political activities, and they were married in 1847. They both joined in the German struggle for constitutional rights, including the publication of a revolutionary newspaper, the *Neue Kölnische Zeitung*.

Mathilde Franziska's earliest writings lack the political elements that her later work shows, starting with "Woman in Conflict with Society." In her discussion of Mathilde Franziska's literary work, Maria Wagner places her work as Mathilde von Tabouillot in the Biedermeier period, while her work as Mathilde Anneke falls clearly under *Vormärz* (*MFA in Selbstzeugnissen* 370). She defines this second type of literature as exhibiting "political activism, socialistic goals, [and] also a certain radicalism" (370, my translation; Wagner cites Helmut Koopmann, *Das Junge Deutschland*, Metzler 1970, 31). It is the political force of the work that matters; as Jost Hermand indicates, these writers were revolutionaries, who often did not concern themselves with stylistic brilliance, who were not focused on the artistic, but rather on a revolutionary call to arms (Wagner 370, my paraphrase; she cites J. Hermand, Hrsg. *Der deutsche Vormärz*, Stuttgart 1967, 364–66).

Although the main focus of this book is on Anneke's writings that included a political purpose, I will include here a brief commentary on her earlier Biedermeier works. Work from this period is often considered imitative and "harmless," and these descriptions would certainly also apply to Mathilde Franziska's work from this period (Wagner, *MFA in Selbstzeugnissen* 367). She was writing in desperate circumstances as a means of earning a living for herself and her daughter. In 1839, her first prayer book, *Des Christen freudigen Aufblick zum himmlischen Vater* (*A Christian's Joyful Look Upward to the Heavenly Father*) appeared, followed in 1841 by *Der Meister ist da und rufet Dich* (*The Lord Is Here and Calls You*) with the subtitle *Ein vollständiges Gebet- und Erbauungsbuch für die katholische Frauenwelt von Mathilde Franziska, verehelicht gewesene Tabouillot, geb. Gießler* (*A Compete Prayer and Devotional Book for Catholic Women by Mathilde Franziska, formerly married as Tabouillot, maiden name Gießler*). These two books served the practical purpose of providing work and income, but also gave expression to her Catholic beliefs and refuge in religion during this difficult time in her life. Such books plus her early poetry, occasionally published in a journal or newspaper, and her short story, "Die Melkerin von Blankenstein" (The Milkmaid of Blankenstein), which appears in *Taschenbuch deutscher Sagen* (*Handbook of German Sagas*; Wagner 367) do not reflect the author's mature work and passion for social change. They are firmly anchored in her time and imitative in theme and style. As Maria Wagner notes in her analysis, Annette von Droste-Hülshoff labeled the poetry as "miserable" and "watery" and called the prose "even worse" (*MFA in Selbstzeugnissen* 367).

In spite of this opinion, Droste-Hülshoff provided three poems for Mathilde Franziska's *Westfälisches Jahrbuch* (1846) *Produkte der Rothen Erde* (*Products of the Red Earth*) (Wagner, *MFA in Selbstzeugnissen* 309). Mathilde Franziska edited three almanacs during this time, including *Heimatgruß* (1840) (*Greeting from the Homeland*) and *Damenalmanach* (1841) (*Almanac for Ladies*) and was able to include the work of several other authors, along with her own. She provided poetry, a short story, a travelogue (*Reisebeschreibung*) entitled "Eine Reise im Mai 1843" (Ruben 12), a biographical piece on the painter Wilhelm Kaulbach, and several translations (Wagner, *MFA in Selbstzeugnissen* 369). The third almanac, the *Westfälisches Jahrbuch*, even used as its motto lines from a poem by Freiligrath, showing the beginnings of political engagement not apparent in the two earlier almanacs.

Early biographer Regina Ruben sees positive characteristics in the two prayer books. She notes that they are not pure formula (*Schablonenarbeit*) but rather a true reflection of the reaction of a woman whose situation gives her no refuge except religion. Ruben sees no blind religiosity (*Frommheit*), but rather submission to God's goodness and mercy (10–11). This writing may well have been Mathilde Franziska's strength in her hour of need, and certainly reflects desperate circumstances, but in later years, she struck through her motto, which referred to longing for heaven and the soul's contemplation and prayer, and wrote: "Von den Göttern, die der Mensch in seiner Not erschuf!" ("From the gods which man created in his need!") (Ruben 11). Ruben follows love as a constant theme in this early work, but at this stage it is still love combined with belief in God and, at least in *Heimatgruß*, submission to authority (*Fürstenverehrung*) (Ruben 11).

Oithono oder die Tempelweihe (1844), her only drama, was also written during her early period. The theme of love is present along with the theme of the artist in conflict with the world. Although not raised to the level of a classic, the drama is one of the few written by a woman (Wagner, *MFA in Selbstzeugnissen* 401) and shows parallels with Goethe's *Tasso* and Franz Grillparzer's *Der Traum ein Leben* (Ruben 399). The dramatic elements and pathos made it successful on stage, both at the opening in Germany, and later in Milwaukee when performed in 1884, Annette von Droste-Hülshoff's harsh criticism of the opening performance notwithstanding (Wagner, *MFA in Selbstzeugnissen* 401–402). Mathilde Franziska's knowledge and love of literature was to be evident throughout her life, although her own work will focus more on political themes, and, as is the case in *Vormärz* literature, social themes will take precedence over artistic form. As she rejects her earlier religious feeling, Mathilde Franziska embraces some of the doubt expressed through her character Oithono and becomes a free thinker and liberal in the revolutionary climate of the mid-1840s.

As Mathilde Franziska moved from the protected world of her childhood and the status provided by her first marriage, she came in contact with the difficult realities of a woman's position in society. Legally, she did not have the same standing as men, and practically, she was less educated and barred from most paid professions. As a woman from the upper class, but now divorced and raising a child alone, there were limited possibilities for her to earn a living. Rejected by the circles of "decent society," she nevertheless enjoyed the stimulating ideas and conversation of a group of intellectual freethinkers, where she could indulge her love of literature. The poet and political activist Ferdinand Freiligrath became a friend and contributed to her almanac, the *Westphalian Yearbook* (*Westfälisches Jahrbuch*). The group also included radical leaders like Karl Marx and a young Prussian officer Fritz Anneke.

During this time, as a result of both personal experience and discussion of liberal political ideas, Mathilde Franziska became more radical in her thinking and abandoned her *Biedermeier*-style writing for the more socially activist literature and essays of the *Vormärz*. One outlet for this writing was the liberal press, including the *Kölnische Zeitung* and the *Augsburger Allgemeine Zeitung* (Möhrmann 222). Fritz Anneke, whom she married on June 3, 1847, had also turned to political writing.

When the Annekes moved from Münster to Cologne, their home remained a center of intellectual and political life. The Worker's Party (*Arbeiter-Verein*), of which Fritz Anneke was a committee member, published its own newspaper, *Zeitung des Arbeiter-Vereines zu Köln*, with the motto, "Freedom, Brotherhood, Work,"[2] and their friend Freiligrath published his famous revolutionary poem, "Die Todten an die Lebenden (Juli 1848)" ("The Dead Address the Living") in the September 7, 1848, issue. On September 10, 1848, the *Neue Kölnische Zeitung* (*New Cologne Newspaper*) appeared with Fritz Anneke and Fritz Beust listed as editors. Their premier issue makes a clear statement of aims, and distinguishes itself from the ("old") *Kölnische Zeitung* by writing that their new newspaper, with its subtitle "Für Bürger, Bauern und Soldaten" (For Citizens, Farmers, and Soldiers), is especially intended for working people. The language is revolutionary and inflammatory, accusing the upper classes—specifically government officials, the nobility, the wealthy, and church leaders—of lying and deceiving the workers. The *Neue Kölnische Zeitung* is intended to replace the old newspaper, which, the editor writes, does not speak for the majority of Cologne's citizens:

> The **old** *Kölnische Zeitung* is a newspaper for men with a sack of gold [*Männer des Geldsacks*]; it has always been an enemy of the working people, and it would like nothing better than to keep them in oppression and slavery [*Knechtschaft*], where they are mired to this present day. The 'New Cologne Newspaper' (like the New Rhineland [Newspaper]) wants the exact opposite; it wants the destruction of the dominance of the sack of gold [*Herrschaft des Geldsackes*] and the **fundamental** improvement of the **entire** living conditions of working people, and we are sure that the 'New Cologne Newspaper' coincides with the opinion of the **great** majority of Cologne's citizens.[3]

The summer before, in June 1848, there was a Congress of Democratic Clubs in Frankfurt, where Fritz Anneke and Cologne Worker's Newspaper editor, Andreas Gottschalk, were delegates. The revolutionary ideas from this Congress, including declaring for a Republic and the continuing debate in Cologne, caused the police to arrest Anneke, Gottschalk, and another member of the society, Joseph Esser. Wisconsin Historical Society archival notes summarize the charges this way:

> All three were accused of a plot for the purpose of overthrowing the government and stirring up a civil war by inducing the citizens to arm against each other, or of inciting them to outrages for such purposes by speeches in public assemblies, by printed writings and posting of placards.[4]

After Fritz Anneke's brutal arrest, Mathilde Franziska kept regular contact with him in jail and produced the *Neue Kölnische Zeitung* on her own (planned to be published daily, except Monday). On September 10, when the first issue appeared, Fritz was under arrest and co-editor Beust supplied funds but was never directly involved in the production of the paper (Henkel 38); therefore, Mathilde Franziska handled all of the activities related to the paper, seeing to the writing, editing, and printing, and was editor in all but name (Gebhardt 71). In fact, Maria Wagner argues convincingly that Mathilde Franziska was the driving force behind this new type of newspaper, written especially for workers, not only in the production, but also in the founding stages (Wagner, *MFA in Selbstzeugnissen* 37). She agrees with Renate Möhrmann's assessment that crediting Fritz Anneke with this newspaper is an example of how a woman's achievements are often hidden under the name of her husband. Mathilde Anneke's letters do indeed reveal a woman of extraordinary courage and strength (See: Wagner, *MFA in Selbstzeugnissen* 39–46), who was quite capable of handling the newspaper and family matters in the absence of her husband, and also to support and encourage him while he was imprisoned. However, fourteen days after the first issue appeared, all democratic organizations and newspapers were forbidden, and this newspaper was also temporarily suspended (Gebhardt 78). Some months later it would again appear on a regular basis, until after the Revolution of 1848 broke out (Wagner, *MFA in Selbstzeugnissen* 38–39). Mathilde Anneke got around the ban by immediately publishing her *Frauenzeitung*, whose first issue appeared on September 27, 1848, with her name listed this time as editor. And, indeed, the paper was totally her project, as Fritz Anneke was still in prison, and Breust, according to the letter to subscribers in her first edition, planned another small newspaper on his own (Wagner, *MFA in Selbstzeugnissen* 44). Two issues of the newspaper appeared before the third was suppressed. Excerpts from Mathilde Anneke's important essay, "Das Weib im Conflict mit den socialen Verhältnissen," which was published in 1847 as a small booklet, appeared in the second issue of her *Frauenzeitung* (Henkel 20). Although not long-lived, this was the first feminist newspaper in Germany (Wagner, "A German Writer..." 161), and the idea of such a newspaper was something she would come back to when she immigrated to America.

Her first issue of *Frauen-Zeitung* from Wednesday, September 27, 1848, explains the temporary ban on the *Neue Kölnische Zeitung*, and promptly continues to publish under this new name. Some have argued that it cannot be counted as a feminist newspaper. Gebhardt, for example, (79) argues that the *Frauen-Zeitung* is not a woman's periodical and certainly not a feminist newspaper. He points out that Mathilde Anneke did not see herself as a women's rights activist [*Frauenrechtlerin*], at least during this time period. As he says, she was acting as a political journalist, who was trying to win both men and women over to the revolutionary cause, recognizing (correctly in his view) that the Revolution of 1848 was a matter involving everyone [*eine Sache des ganzen Volkes*], not just the men.

However, as Wagner points out in her article on Anneke, "A German Writer and Feminist in 19th-Century America," the aim of the paper was "to agitate for equal rights for women through education and to free women from the influence of the church" (161). Indeed, her front-page article, entitled "Kirche und Schule" ("Church and School"), deals with church control of children's education. In direct fashion, she sketches the origins of early church control over education in the monasteries, when monks were the only available teachers. She argues that things have changed and notes harshly that this is "because people gradually came to the conclusion that monks and nuns were merely lazy *Gesindel* (rabble), who lived at the expense of other people."[5] However, the church wished to maintain control over schooling. Anneke continues: "All enlightened people have now come to the conclusion that school must be separated from church; that is, that the priesthood should no longer maintain control [*Aufsicht* = oversight] over the schools because, first of all, it is not their business (area of expertise), and, second, that it harms instruction." She argues that reading, writing, and arithmetic do not have a particularly Christian dimension. "Are there virtuous, Christian

ABCs…?" she asks. Indeed, Anneke believes strongly that so much church influence over women and children guarantees a system of "liars and hypocrites," and suggests that church control keeps people from using their reason to determine what is best.

From this early newspaper article, the reader can already hear the voice of the committed political activist who will argue for women's right to vote. This particular question, namely the influence of the church in the rearing of children, was a topic of considerable discussion at that time in Cologne. Anneke addresses herself to the people actually raising their children and hopes to influence society, starting with the individual.

As noted above, Gebhardt argued that the *Frauen-Zeitung* was not a "feminist" newspaper, while Wagner points to the aims of the paper to promote women's rights, a point of view that today would clearly qualify as "feminist." The disagreement revolves, in part, around the use of the term "feminist" itself, which is a source of controversy even today. In most cases, I will avoid calling Anneke a feminist, and yet to give her credit for her journalistic accomplishments, I find the usage unavoidable when referring to her newspapers, and completely in line with the usage of historians tracing the development of the feminist press. To refer to Anneke herself, however, I take into account Nancy F. Cott's position on the usage of this terminology as expressed in *The Grounding of Modern Feminism*. In the introduction, Cott points out that "[p]eople in the nineteenth century did not say *feminism*. They spoke of the advancement of woman or the cause of woman, woman's rights, and woman suffrage. Most inclusively, they spoke of the woman movement, to denote the many ways women moved out of their homes to initiate measures of charitable benevolence, temperance, and social welfare and to instigate struggles for civic rights, social freedoms, higher education, remunerative occupations, and the ballot. Nineteenth-century women's consistent usage of the singular *woman* symbolized, in a word, the unity of the female sex. It proposed that all women have one cause, one movement" (3). The term *feminism* was used first in the 1910s to supplant the archaic-sounding "woman movement" and came to denote a set of principles beyond the suffrage movement. The new usage proclaimed a revolution in the relations of the sexes and "marked the end of the woman movement and the embarkation on a modern agenda" (4). Because the words *feminist* and *feminism* relate to this new agenda,[6] and because Mathilde Anneke is clearly a nineteenth-century activist, shaped by her own times and culture, I prefer to call her just that, an activist, even while recognizing the early historical importance of her newspapers to later feminism.

Mathilde Anneke was as devoted to the revolutionary movement in Germany as her husband was. The ideas expressed in her newspaper so fervently were clearly hers, and her actions followed her words. When Fritz Anneke was released from prison, he joined the revolutionary army as an officer, and Mathilde followed him into battle, serving with Carl Schurz as his aide-de-camp (Wagner, "A German Writer...161). She later published an account of her experiences entitled *Memoiren einer Frau aus dem badisch-pfälzischen Feldzüge* (*Memoirs of a Woman from the Baden-Palatinate Campaign*).[7] Anneke endured ridicule from the "old" *Kölnische Zeitung* for taking on this role. The biographical notes of Henrietta M. Heinzen in the Wisconsin Historical Society archives report the situation as follows:

> The aged General Sznaide, seasoned in the Polish revolution and the campaigns of Napoleon, greeted the charming "orderly" as an Amazon, but came off badly. Her intention was not to carry arms, but to make herself useful as a woman, and with difficulty her husband urged upon her a pistol for protection. Not without just sensitiveness Mathilde Franziska Anneke relates how the old Koelnische Zeitung represented her as wearing a fantastic costume. "A weighty sword, a cutlass, a musket and men's clothing are the requisites which they also had ready for me out of their chest of lies—while I took part in the campaign at the side of my husband, unarmed and in my usual costume, which was merely turned into a riding habit by means of linen trousers." She had not expected that those men, who had known her from childhood and with whom she had been on friendly and literary relations, would accuse her of "so ridiculous an exaggeration." (18)

As Wagner's article, "A German Writer and Feminist in 19th-Century America," makes clear, the fact that Anneke fought alongside her husband during the Revolution of 1848 in Germany gave her special prominence on at least two occasions later in her life. On one occasion in 1853 at the national women's rights convention in New York, a mob tried to keep her from speaking, but she refused to yield. Abolitionist Wendell Phillips declared to the mob that "Mrs. Anneke felt no fear in [the] face of this vulgar outburst since she had defied even cannon-fire in the cause for freedom" (169).[8] She was able to finish her speech. On a second occasion she was lobbying in Washington in 1870 with a committee who hoped to have legislation introduced to Congress allowing women in the District of Columbia to vote. The report in *The History of Woman Suffrage* (Vol. 2, 425, cited in Wagner, "A

German Woman Writer and Feminist" 172) reminds the reader that Anneke spoke with great emotion on the question, and that "the burden of it all was that the trials of the battlefield were as naught as compared to this inward struggle of her soul toward liberty for women."

Her experiences in Germany had transformed the young woman of the *Biedermeier* period into a revolutionary. She was already an activist when she arrived on American shores. She was to have a great deal of success with her lectures during her career, but perhaps her most dramatic moment came at the famous Mob Convention in New York, September 6 and 7, 1853, which was mentioned at the end of Chapter 1 of this book. In *The History of Woman Suffrage*, Vol. 1, it is reported in the table of contents under the title, "Mob in the Broadway Tabernacle Woman's Rights Convention through two days, 1853." In the view of Stanton, Anthony, and Gage, the attitude of the leading newspapers, with the exception of *The Tribune*, encouraged "the mob element" to interrupt the Woman's Rights Convention with "shouts, hisses, stamping, and cheers, rude remarks, and all manner of noisy demonstrations." The result was, in their words: "The clergy, the press, and the rowdies combined to make those September days a disgrace to the metropolis, days never to be forgotten by those who endured the ridicule and persecution" (547). The weapon of ridicule was a particularly effective one against women of the nineteenth century, who were especially vulnerable to this type of attack against their reputations and standing in society.

This was Anneke's first Convention, but she had endured ridicule in the form of personal attacks against her in the German press; so she was familiar with this weapon. She also had no intention of sitting on the sidelines. The report of this Convention includes a resolution with the intent of spreading the members' activism overseas. The full text reads: "*Resolved*, That inasmuch as this great movement is intended to meet the wants, not of America only, but of the whole world, a committee be appointed to prepare an address from the Convention to the women of Great Britain and the continent of Europe, setting forth our objects, and inviting their co-operation in the same" (Stanton, Anthony, & Gage, *The History of Woman Suffrage* 570). The committee included well-known suffragists like Lucretia Mott, Lucy Stone, and Elizabeth Blackwell, as well as both Ernestine L. Rose and Mathilde Franziska Anneke.

Anneke's speech is indicative of her tremendous oratory power and persuasiveness. Ernestine L. Rose translated for her, as she had not been in the United States very long and was more comfortable speaking in German. Indeed, throughout her life, Anneke was much more at home in her native language than in English, and many of her speeches and lectures were to German-American audiences and given in German. Her remarks on this occasion are reported in *The History of Woman Suffrage* (572). I have included the full text of that speech in Chapter 6 in my discussion of Anneke's contributions to the movement for women's rights, where I also include several of her writings, including another planned speech related to the suffrage issue. The purpose of these remarks was to contrast the right to freedom of speech in America with the lack of freedoms in Germany, and Anneke verbally confronted the hecklers who would deny her the opportunity to speak. As a revolutionary Forty-Eighter, her hopes for a German republic were connected with freedom of speech and freedom of the press. The fact that her own newspaper had been shut down by the censors, and, of course, the experience of Fritz Anneke's arrest, both had reinforced her belief in the power of free people expressing their opinions. She was reluctant to come and speak to the convention, due to illness and even more her lack of English, but it is clear that her sympathies lay with the cause of women's rights, and she was finally persuaded to come. Her passionate words illustrated how much the United States served as "illustration and example" for those fighting to change Germany. The resolution that offered to join with Europe in the common cause was a tremendous encouragement to her, and she immediately became politically active in her new country, just as she had been in Germany. Her thoughts at this early date are especially strongly connected to her homeland as she concludes: "The women of my country look to this for encouragement and sympathy; and they, also, sympathize with this cause. We hope it will go on and prosper; and many hearts across the ocean in Germany are beating in unison with those here" (*The History of Woman Suffrage* 572).

Notes

1. Spelling as cited from a letter by Annette von Droste-Hülshoff, cited by M. Wagner in *Mathilde Franziska Anneke in Selbstzeugnissen und Dokumenten*.

2. Pages 1 and 2 of issue number 29 from Thursday, September 7, 1848, are available in the Anneke Archives of the Wisconsin Historical Society in Madison.

3. My translation is from page 2 of the *Neue Kölnische Zeitung*, No. 1, Sonntag, den 10. September 1848. Original emphasis in bold letters has been retained. This text also cited in Henkel, page 39.

4. Biographical Notes in Commemoration of Fritz Anneke and Mathilde Franziska Giesler Anneke by Henrietta M. Heinzen (Anneke Collection, Madison, Wisconsin).

5. My translation of Anneke's text in German. All of Anneke's writings are originally in German, and I use my own translation unless otherwise indicated.

6. Cott includes three components in her definition (pages 4–5): (1) sex equity or "opposition to one sex's categorical control of the rights and opportunities of the other," (2) the presumption that women's condition is socially constructed rather than predestined, and (3) the proposition that women see themselves "not only as a biological sex but (perhaps even more importantly) as a social grouping."

7. The original text was published in Newark, New Jersey, by the Buchdruckerei Fritz Anneke in 1853. The text is reprinted in Henkel, 63–121.

8. A full description of this incident can be found on page 512ff of Stanton et al., *The History of Woman Suffrage*, Vol. 1.

Chapter 3

Louise Aston and "Woman in Conflict with Society"

"Woman in Conflict with Society" was Mathilde Franziska Anneke's first major essay on the subject of improving the lot of women. Although the title refers to a specific woman, Louise Aston, in conflict with nineteenth-century German society, Anneke's purpose in writing the piece goes beyond her immediate legal case. This essay was written on the eve of the Revolution of 1848, or in her own words, "in the winter before the Revolution 1846–1847," when German liberals were fighting for more participation in their own government. Anneke, a committed Forty-Eighter, saw herself and other women as also deserving of rights. In this context, the societal position allotted to women angered her and stimulated her to write a scathing essay as a wake-up call to women suffering under the yoke of oppressive law and custom. The stimulus for this essay was, in the first place, an actual case that shocked many of her time: the exile of Louise Aston from Berlin on the basis of her opinions. Anneke lays out the circumstances and the specific case, but her main interest goes beyond the fate of an individual woman. The treatment of Louise Aston is, to Anneke, clear evidence of the intolerable circumstances under which women lived. Indeed, Ruth-Ellen Boetcher Joeres suggests in her book, *Respectability and Deviance*, that the ambivalence found in Aston's life and works might represent "the near futility of open rebellion under the unfavorable conditions presented by the fate of being an outspoken woman in Germany in the nineteenth century" (117).[1]

Anneke's own experience with her first marriage, as we have seen, was not so different from Aston's and her empathy may well have come from that experience. As long as a woman was fortunate in her marriage and able to accept the sphere given her, she could ignore the societal structures that kept her from developing as a full human being. A divorced woman, regardless of her intelligence and character, was automatically looked down on as not quite acceptable in polite society. The stigma of a failed marriage was hers, not her ex-husband's. When the economic difficulties faced by women trying to earn a living are added to the social disapproval of divorce, it is clear that societal constraints were not set up to protect women but were instead a great detriment. Anneke, like Aston, was a strong, intelligent woman for whom such a system was no longer acceptable. Her defense of Aston is the first of her writings in the area of women's rights and foreshadows her later activity in the Woman Suffrage Movement when she moved to the United States.

The full text of her essay "Das Weib im Conflict mit den socialen Ver-haeltnissen" ("Woman in Conflict with Society") [2] is translated here:

It was probably somewhat longer than a year before the March Revolution when a unique case joined the famous Prussian expulsion story—that spiteful proceeding of the Berlin police against Mr. Itzstein and Mr. Hacker—namely *the expulsion of a woman*.[3] *Louise Aston* was her name, a pretty, young, unfortunate woman, a writer and the poor divorced wife of a rich man. The newspapers did not refrain from exploiting this unusual case in their customary way and supplied completely contradictory statements about the fate of this woman, who, because of her free opinions and way of thinking, seemed dangerous to the police of a capital city. The actual motives, which supposedly led to such a high-profile proceeding, were reported very differently, and even if their truth were proven, they would not justify the action taken. No one could get a true picture [of the situation] from the contradictions in these reports, and from the talk going around about the exiled woman; however, these were all the more inclined to awaken interest and sympathy for her in the hearts of everyone, but especially in the hearts of women. No chivalrous knight, with the sharp weapon of free speech, stepped forward publicly in defense of this wronged woman, even though it was said that a man of princely family and rank, endowed with wealth and honor, had wooed her in vain. People knew that a contemporary singer had dedicated his song to her, that thinking men stood around the cell where she suffered and wrote—and yet there was no one who, at the moment of her banishment, broke his lance for her with the courtliness of medieval romanticism—no one who raised a word of defense for her loudly and clearly with the fire of truth and conviction—no one who, with all the eloquence of our reporters, could give believable information in response to our question: "What possible crime has this woman committed?"

In the meantime, a small cycle of her own poems had appeared [a typed footnote identifies the work as *Wilde Rosen, Gedichte von Louise Aston* (*Wild Roses, Poems by Louise Aston*). Berlin bei W. Moeser & Kuehn, 1846.]. The poet called her twelve songs *Wild Roses*, which sprang from the wild, wild ground of a feminine heart, growing luxuriantly around a destroyed life and love story, sending forth tendrils, and which she greeted with the words:

> "In the freedom of wild display,
> Rocked to sleep by the roar of the storm
> Nursed on dew at the end of the day."

No white rose, delicate and sensible, blooms under the dew of silent womanly tears in her poetic breast and exhales fragrance for us from the bouquet. No—deep and dark, burning roses, each carrying in its outer cup the heavy drop of blood of a painfully struggling, fatally bleeding heart—they *blaze* toward us with their dark misery, from which the buds suddenly escaped.

From these twelve poems by *Louise Aston*, we get to know the woman who was forced to give herself to a man without love; who in the boisterous tones of song, threw down her curse against "*a holy festival*," whose ceremony more fortunate women celebrate in our time with joyful devotion, by bringing the sacred myrtle[4] to the sacrificial flame of their domestic altar. We see her breaking her chains, plunging in her flight deeper and deeper into the endless depths of a despairing sorrow, and ordaining herself as sorrow's priestess. Then we find her in jail, shrouded in dark "imaginings," struggling in their spiritual grip, and disdaining salvation, the promise of which the open Bible in front of her reminded her; we find her lost in wild "*Dionysian songs*," with bacchanalian spirits of an unchained life hovering and dancing around her; we find her yielding to reveling dreams, from which she awakens with a loudly lamenting hymn "*To George Sand*," a heroic woman in whom she saw the liberation of [her] downtrodden sex. Finally we hear her openly confess her "*life motto*":

> To a life of freedom and love's free ways
> Have I devoted myself always—
> [Freiem Lieben, freiem Leben/Hab ich ewig mich ergeben—]

With such a confession, for which, in its frank point of view, the poet will never be forgiven by harmless women, the struggle within her heart is ended, and she appears to us after this struggle in the following poem, "Harmonie." A woman is born again to love, to that love which we all gladly praise:[5]

> 'Tis day which dawns shining!
> No longer does confused dream hold me prisoner!
> The phantoms around me I see disperse,
> Overflowing into the wide sea of light
> Sonorously has harmony pierced my heart
> A great and honest feeling has overcome me.
> To him I grant joyously the right of conquest.
> He shall remain my lord forever,
> Let every pulse beat be the victor's slave;
> My whole soul will I yield to him!
> --------------
>
> Oh, sweet pain, to clamor so for freedom!
> Oh, sweet servitude, to wear such chains!
> Warlike feelings and thoughts,
> Which boldly challenged the world to battle,
> The free spirit's defiant vassals
> Now have fallen powerlessly to the new spell!
> *Unhappy* was I, when I was master,
> And proudly played with desires and impulses;
> Yet *happiness* surrounds me sweet and wonderful,
> *Since I yielded my whole soul to him.*
> --------------
>
> Once earth's richest goods were mine,
> The pride, the joy of foolish spirits!
> Given to the arrogance of youth,
> I dared to dally with all of life!
> In my frivolous game I felt the weight of existence,
> In full richness the emptiness of my heart!
> My feelings were given away, empty were my senses,
> And only a strong longing remained in me;
> *Till I gave my All to the One*
> *Till I yielded my whole soul to him.*

However, only once does the harmony of her soul ring in full tones in her song; soon she is again torn by the harsh dissonance of her former sorrow. The longing for self-sacrificing love is not stilled in real union, and this is the surge, in which the stormy floods of a burning heart are dashed to pieces. She cannot flee the memory of lost days, which have destroyed her youth and her joy. She struggles with the pain which will not let her free. She *is supposed* to smile, and no one knows that that can only happen with bitter tears. She *is supposed* to appear happy, and no one suspects that she, a cypress, laments at the grove of the vanished dreams of her youth:

> Can I lessen this longing
> Which unites me in dreams with you?
> Hateful to you are these tears
> Which pale grief cries!
> Very well…I will painfully struggle,
> To master [my] dark sadness:
> In order to bury its dead,
> Let the dead themselves strive;
> Still, may life's best fortune
> Smile on the living!
> ["Kann ich lindern dieses Sehen
> Dass mich traeumend Dir vereint?
> Dir verhasst sind diese Thraenen,
> Die der blasse Kummer weint!
> Wol.. so will ich schmerzhaft ringen,
> Finstre Trauer zu bezwingen:
> Ihre Todten zu begraben,
> Lass die Todten sich bemuehen;
> Doch des Lebens reichste Gaben,
> Moegen dem Lebendgen bluehen!"]

Well then, what was left for her? For her, the ailing woman, to whom the world was a jail, in which she lay chained by her burning wishes? "*A Last Comfort*," her whole achievement, whose salvation is only this:

> From the depths of one's own thoughts,
> From the embers of one's own soul,
> Like the noble Arabian steed

> To bleed to death from open veins.
> ["An des eignen Gedankens Geschoss,
> An der eignen Seele Gluten,
> Wie das edle arabische Ross
> An geoeffneten Adern verbluten."]

Her confused "night fantasies" conclude the dark and ghastly round dance of these twelve songs. From them we derive absolutely no hope for the poor, errant woman, for the unhappy night wanderer. We see clearly that she stands before a dangerous precipice; she will inevitably fall in, if a tender dawn of love does not lead her gently back, and if its pure light does not sink into her stormy heart with its healing shine.

A poetic work of art does not usually give us a clear picture of the object which it treats. However, from the poems just analyzed, this time we have gotten more than a *hint* of a failed life and a failed love; we have gathered almost the *certainty* of a completely lost happiness in life. And in this certainty, there is for us hardly even a slight hope of saving such a rich and shattered woman. Therefore we place all memory of her in a coffin along with our many dead.

We almost thought that her "*Wild Roses*" already had their grave mound without blooming, when suddenly a strong glimmer of life flashes from the heart believed dead. It pulses and penetrates through all living spirits and wakens them for battle; not to bloody battle, the hand of a woman never grasps the sword. No longer a pale apparition does she appear ghostlike in our nights—no, an active, lively woman steps outside her boundaries and accuses the threatening power simply, loudly, and clearly. There appears by her a small book, *My Emancipation, Banishment, and Justification*, which provides the most compelling evidence of this woman's oppression on the part of the authorities. Since this book's publication,[6] not one single public contradiction has been offered to any of the facts presented in it. Therefore, we are all the more fully justified in giving her report complete credibility. This small contribution has done more for [women's] history than all the defenders, who have ever thrown themselves into the fray for the downtrodden sex and have had an influence in so many different ways.

In her booklet,[7] Louise Aston brings, in part, the fate of her public life to the attention of an open form. To go into her inner frame of mind before a public forum, she does not feel herself called upon for the present. In this case, it is also merely a question of pleading for the position of women within society because, since even this has been denied her, since the reviled woman herself no longer finds a rock upon which to lay down her tired head, it is mainly a question of defending openly her public rights against the powers of this world and to vindicate herself against the charges raised.

Why, after all, should woman continue to be the silent sufferer? Why continue to be the humble maid, "who washes the feet of her lord?" *Why* continue to be the humble Christian maid of a lord who has become a *tyrant* over her heart because he himself is a *slave*?

The voice of this small book awakened many slumbering women who were not yet too deep in sleep from the bubbling of their cooking pot on the hearth. She called many a quiet bearer, who struggles bleeding under the yoke of societal misery, which weighs upon women's hearts unnoticed and unrecognized, [she called them] to consciousness of the ultimate power of their dying strength so that they might pull themselves together and take courage, if only to, at least, complain loudly of their fate. She poured courage into their timid souls to shake the fortresses of the old, whitewashed temple, which is decorated with the myrtle of sacrificed brides, and makes a show of the outward holiness of thousands of inwardly broken marriage ties—and even if it is only to shake a single stone of this decaying structure.

Louise Aston gives us her story in the short telling of her exile, after she defended herself from being considered frivolous. The extreme *necessity* justifies the step of publishing her private business; to oppose such a step out of false feelings of shame, she rightly considered *cowardly* and *dishonorable*.

Louise was the daughter of a Lutheran clergyman, Church Councilman *Hoche* in Groeningen. As a very young girl, she was married to a rich English factory owner, Mr. Aston, a man whom she did not love. In this marriage, she lived surrounded by *glamour* and *riches*, but *without* love. Young, beautiful, and rich, she entered into the grand life, but she found herself alone and unhappy. Here she got to know modern life in all its conflicts and contradictions, and, she tells us, she "also soon [got to know] the powerful antithesis, which destroys a woman's heart and threatens some day to turn the basic order of society upside down, the antithesis between love and marriage, affection and duty, heart and conscience."

The marriage ended in divorce. Do not despise her for that, you women who learned to accustom yourselves to a "happiness" for which you really never yearned within your youthful ardent breast. Understand that your fictitious happiness has turned you into a *smiling slave*; you have become unfeeling toward others and toward yourself because you no longer feel the scorpion which gnaws on your own heart and cheats you of your heart's best blood. You call *happiness* what is never more than a *shadow of happiness*. Do not despise the woman who broke the chains of your oath sanctified by your false deities—who left the opulent rooms behind her and entered the small chambers of her silent poverty in order to spend her year of mourning in chaste widowhood at the bier of her past youthful happiness. Oh, do not despise her if, instead of wasting her rich life in luxuriously numbing pleasures, she preferred to enter into life, into serious life, to risk and to struggle with it,—if she no longer committed hypocritical betrayal against herself and love, but instead fled—fled from falsehood and its illusion.

We do not know what she has suffered in recognizing what *love is* and what *love is not*. The ardent sighs of her heaving breast we did not witness, the tortures of burning misery we did not experience—but she cries out to us: "From the safety of the shore, the storm is easily exorcised and scorned, with which the unsteady ship fights in vain on the open sea. I have felt deeply what the prophetic voice of George Sand proclaimed to future generations; the suffering of the time, the cry of pain of the victims, which the unnaturalness of relationships torture to death. I know what degradation a woman is subjected to under the sacred protection of the law and of custom; how these helpful household deities[8] turn into useless scarecrows, and how the power of the staff officer becomes brutal force!"

So again: her marriage ended in divorce. Louise Aston moved with her daughter, a four-year-old child, to Berlin, the city of intellectual activity and aspiration, to dedicate herself there to a literary occupation. On the one hand, she hoped to be able to rise above her fate through free intellectual activity; on the other, she wanted to try to ensure, through her own efforts, her independence in regard to material needs. Only a small yearly allowance, hardly enough to maintain a paltry existence for her and her child, was given to her in the divorce settlement, but even this, as small as it was, was not furnished to her by her ex-husband. Therefore, she was forced by pressing needs and privation to take legal proceedings against him to require payment. In addition, as we learn from later authentic communications, she became involved in various conflicts with the court. Because of her opinions, which she never expressed in such a baroque way as the slanderous rumors eagerly spread around, the custody of her child was to be taken away from her; therefore a guardianship suit was brought against her. Furthermore, the unsuccessful attempt to abduct the daughter of this tormented mother gave rise to a criminal charge against her [ex-]husband and his accomplices.

Louise Aston has been subjected to indescribable suffering and fear. The worst thing, however, which could happen to her in her current circumstances was exile from the capital, her residence until now.

At that time in Prussia it often happened that men were exiled from the state because of lèse-majesté,[9] because of evading the censorship laws, or even because of a diplomatic intrigue which someone fearfully thought he saw. It was an everyday occurrence that fallen women were banished from the city walls because of their morally loose activities, for which they neglected to pay a bribe to the royal tax assessors. However, that a woman from the so-called educated classes, a citizen in her own state, could be exiled from its capital city, exiled because of a point of view, a way of thinking—that was something so astonishing—yes, that was an abnormality, a one-of-a-kind situation. After such an occurrence, what else could we expect from the "world," from the standard of our best society than that they would pitilessly condemn a "divorced" woman, now further a *despised exile*, without having beforehand examined the guilty verdict—that they would now completely slander the poor creature, whispering and full of scorn, unmoved by how she lies there on the ground, trampled and broken. What does this matter to the narrow-minded souls of our orthodox moralizers, who have already held their secret trial, and who now only wrinkle their noses when they hear her name mentioned. Indeed, there are sufficient grounds that the *name* alone is outlawed and despised—not only by public opinion—no, made public anathema by "reason of state and law"—through an unprecedented action!

And yet we do not wish to offend these paragons of virtue of our tolerant Christian society. Restrained by the pressure of circumstances, nourished from a young age by *pre*judices, they are not permitted to do otherwise—indeed, they *can no longer* judge [for themselves] *after* [hearing] the facts.[10] This whole caste of our human race, to which they belong exclusively, lies incurably ill from these circumstances. This caste has been nourished for longer than a millennium on superstition and self-denial—and from such a group we are to expect a healthy, independent judgment?

The story of Louise's exile is, in short, the following:

After she had stayed for a year in Berlin, she was required, according to the usual rules, to renew her residence card. The already expired card was handed over to her upon her arrival in Berlin without any difficulties by the police. Instead of obtaining the card requested from the presidium authorities, she received the oral communication of a police officer that the card would not be extended because "anonymous" letters about her had been received by the presidium, indeed even by the king. She was accused in these letters of *having frequented the most indecent society of gentlemen, of having founded a club of emancipated women, and furthermore of not believing in God.* Also against her was the dedication of two love songs by *Gottschall*:[11] "*Madonna and Magdalena*," in which similar tendencies were celebrated, [and] whose objectionable qualities the critics in newspapers for literary entertainment have demonstrated in the clearest possible manner.

As a result of this oral information, Mrs. Aston wrote to the chief of police, explained that her *beliefs* and *opinions* were *her own business* and did not concern anyone else, and that those anonymous letters could only have come from a personal enemy. Since it was most desirable for her to continue to remain a resident of *ethical* Berlin, she asked them to grant her residence there.

Thereupon she was requested to call on the presidium in person. While she was told that Privy Councillor von Luedemann, who would have to rule on her matter, was for the moment busy elsewhere, his deputy, Mr. Stahlschmidt, spoke politely with Mrs. Aston with great tactfulness. Mr. St [Stahlschmidt] cleverly brought the conversation around to *religion* and *marriage*, and Louise was naïve enough to state her innermost opinions about both in front of him.

Imagine her surprise when she was brought into Mr. Von Luedemann's office after the conversation was over, and a protocol was placed before her for a signature, with the words: "this is the confession of faith of Madame Aston"! The conversation conducted with Mr. Stahlschmidt, which was placed before her in the protocol, was written down without her having had the slightest suspicion. She herself, the non-believer, accuses herself of all too great credulity because, after some persuasion and assurances by seemingly credible people that "it would certainly not harm her cause, if she signed that protocol," she actually did sign.

Through this device, the authorities had obtained proof, on the basis of which the verbal order was given to her during her personal appearance before the police: "[She must] leave Berlin within a week because she expressed, and wishes to carry out, ideas which are dangerous to civil peace and order."

Instinctively, we cannot refrain from getting to know better the dreams of a woman, [which are] so dangerous to the state, [and] to which those in the capital of the mighty kingdom of Prussia attribute such great importance. Therefore we ask: "what could this confession of belief of Mrs. Aston's have contained that was so bad that the authorities obtained through the statement of it enough evidence in hand to justify carrying out their intention?"

From the conversation during her personal audience before Minister von Bodelschwingh, which was reported in dialog form in her small brochure, we conclude that the main offense Mrs. Aston gave lies in the fact that she expressed her *religious* feelings freely and aloud. After His Excellency first reproached her for having behaved in such an indecent and unusual manner that it was surprising that she could dare to protest her exile; after she responds that she does not know what His Excellency calls "indecent"—the latter, without engaging in further discussion, asks her: Why she places at the start of her confession of faith that she does not believe in God? She answers: *Because she is not a hypocrite.*

I am not conversant enough with the history of philosophy to be able to cite all the *men*, especially in modern philosophy from Francis Bacon to Spinoza, from Spinoza to Hegel, from Hegel to Feuerbach, who for centuries have not only been allowed to express the results of their research, thought, and knowledge freely and without restraint, but also to *teach* about them publicly. Of course, I have never heard that any of them, while under the power of Christian jurisdiction, had freely confessed that they had overcome almighty God. *Doubts* about this God's personal existence awaken every day, even in the hearts of believing women; I know that thousands suspect, feel, indeed understand, that they have only been handed toys in the form of sacred rosaries and the other symbols of faith. They may *seem* satisfied to imagine nothing but poetic fairy tales in the holy scriptures—however, I know of none who has, through experience and study, arrived at the point of being able to confess aloud with boldness and courage:

"I believe in neither a personal God nor a universal spirit—I know that the happiness promised to us cannot be found in the heavens beyond the stars, but here, here below on the green, flowering earth."

Why is such a confession from the mouth of a woman so very strongly forbidden? Why should the truth remain hidden from *women*, truth, which is the inheritance of our time, and which, in the struggle with falsehood, is beginning to rise victoriously above it? Why do opinions, which men have been allowed to hold for centuries, seem so very dangerous to a state when held *by women*? Could it be because they have in their hands, more than men do, the power of spreading these views, and by being widespread, the views threaten to shake the modern world and governmental order? Could it be because they nourish with their heart's blood stronger belief in a new type of humanity, and can hand down to you in the following generation a healthier, freer race of people who will never become lowly slaves to be sold? *Is that why*? Yes, it is the reason; because, carried by women, the truth, which will overthrow the thrones and altars of tyrants and despots, is emerging victorious. Because only the truth will make us free and release us from the bonds of self-denial, from the chains of slavery. Because the truth frees us from the deceitful illusion that we will be rewarded above for our love and suffering, for our patience and servitude; because the truth brings us to the realization that we have the same rights to the enjoyment of life as our oppressors; that they are the ones who made the laws and gave them to us, not for our good, but for theirs, for their benefit. Because the truth shatters these law tablets, from this time on stands there as victor and need never again be the worried fugitive who knocks on every door, and who can take refuge nowhere. Because, as soon as women's hearts are completely opened to it, eternal refuge is prepared for this truth, and its inheritance is won for humanity.

And the day has come when truth knocks on your hearts. Open them wide, and take part in the inheritance given to you and your children. Do not be deceived any longer! You are so if you do not grasp this possession courageously with your own hands. They want to cloud your senses with the fragrance of incense, delude you with smooth talk, [and] hand you fairy tales wrapped in flowery aroma in place of the simple truth. Clever singers have known how to coo sweet-sounding lullabies to your vigilance and thought, and to praise devotion on the face of women with melodious tones. And this devotion—I say to you—is nothing but hypocrisy and lies with a halo, on which tears of resignation, of misery and unhappiness, indeed tears of privation, grief, and affliction sparkle, trembling like diamonds!

Devotion, this hypocrisy and lies with a halo, has made woman into a dreamer, and in devotion she squanders her passion. She dreams away her strength, which is essential to a fresh, active life. In devotion, this vague longing of the spirit, she has had to stop thinking; oh, it has always been forbidden for woman to think—she has had to stop trying what is good and searching out the best, she has even had to stop taking action! In blind submission, she has left herself to fate alone. And she calls this *"fate"* the "wise decree of a God," this "blind chance" she calls the "higher power," which is supposed to lovingly govern over her!! Oh, open your eyes and see how they have toyed with you; yes, open your eyes; then you will see how you are continually deceived, how there is contradiction in everything which they taught and offered you.

I will be severely rebuked because I dared to question the weak womanly soul's only trust—not in her God—no, in her false deities; because I threatened to overturn on them the foundation upon which they could lean in all of life's troubles and storms. I will be reproached because I stirred up doubts, nothing but doubts, and then as a consequence this nameless despair.

Whoever says she is happy and stands fast, must be *so certain* that she can only mock me smiling in her happiness. *This* mockery, however, does not offend me; if there is still *one* happy, self-assured woman, then with *her* my mission is over. My words are directed only to you unhappy women, only to you, who found a pitiful substitute in faith—and precisely the fact that you could be shaken in this faith by my weak words, provides the best evidence for their genuineness, for the power of their comfort, for your happiness built on a foundation of sand. What I simply and openly and in the most compressed length have expressed here as my confession, has been said hundreds of times by others, more thoroughly and with more proof; however, it did not get through to you because it was said in a language which is only understood by the select few who stand there as if they were high priests in the temple of knowledge.

An *interpretation* of these high priests and learned writers was provided to us, but the true, the simple clear *understanding* was withheld from us! All of us were not supposed to penetrate the sanctuary and know the truth, which now also grips women's hearts with power, and calls on us to tear away the curtain with courageous hands.

Behind that curtain lies the open book which teaches conviction of the truth. Therefore do not trust your superficial understanding alone at this moment; *gain conviction* of the truth, and through it help vigorously to prepare that work for humanity. Do not suppose, mothers and women, that I set too great store by your support! Do not suppose that I have become [so] enraptured with the prevailing ideas of our time that I impose the concerns for that noble work, the efforts and toil related to it upon your weak womanly shoulders, and proclaim the solution of the fate of the world with *you*! Oh, see your babies, you mothers, resting in your arms! Do you want to continue nursing them with the milk of lies? Do you not wish to strengthen them already at your breast with the healthy breath of the new intellectual-spiritual spring,[12] and prepare them for the sacred reception of complete truth? *It is up to you* to make them susceptible to the *truth* or—to *lies*; up to you to lead the *free* son to the *free* father so that he can complete what and how you have begun! *It is up to you* to raise daughters who will never favor a slave with their smile!

One is indebted to the great mothers of antiquity and their *spiritual care* of their children for the great men of that time: Epaminondas[13] is proof of that debt, as are Tiberius Gracchus and Gaius Sempronius Gracchus.[14] Mothers, let our times give similar proof!

With admirable eloquence, Louise Aston has presented in general terms in the above-mentioned book her ideas about women's emancipation, "for which she expresses devoted longing." What woman shall hereafter not hope, with her, for the fulfillment of this longing? The frank confession of her beliefs and opinions, her thorough vindication in the face of the proceedings of the Berlin authorities, awakened a special sympathy in the women and men of our time. We had the right to set upon her the boldest expectations; we longed for every expression of her clear view of current matters with the fresh, new energy of this brave woman.

Then she appears to us in person! In the form of a novel,[15] she appears before us in her whole personality, with her inner feelings and outside experiences. What a painful impression this appearance gives us! How many of our hopes are dashed by this publication!

We know that she presents herself as heroine of this *Fragment from Her Life*. She is herself *Johanna*, the girl endowed with irresistible beauty; *she* is the wife sold to Mr. *Oburn*, a man whom *she* portrays with the most repugnant qualities of appearance as well as of character.

Thus the author, through her skilled portrayal, summons in us the deepest sympathy for Johanna, whose father, a heartless country clergyman, forces his daughter into accepting a marriage contract with the rich English factory owner Oburn. She transports us to indignation over the power of a barbaric father over his child—then she immediately destroys our sympathy and our developing honor and love for her again in blind vanity, in an obvious lack of womanly delicacy of feeling and nobility. In the harshest contrasts, the author holds the portrayal of her own personality, which she finds very pleasing, up to that very displeasing [personality] of the husband who has, I admit, been forced on the poor girl; this portrayal awakens angry distrust within us, indeed she almost forces upon us the conviction of her spiteful bias, unworthy of a woman's heart. She shows no evidence of the nobility of a calm character which clearly comprehends the circumstances in this woman who, instead of throwing the blame upon the contemptible *institutions* of our society, is placed so hostilely in opposition to the *people*, who are led and have been raised by these institutions. The author had not yet raised herself to *the* spiritual freedom, which a person needs to understand personal misfortune, and to separate it from *her own misfortune*, in order to be able to present such misfortune critically and skillfully as more evidence for the unspeakable misery which especially the female sex is subject to under the present disorder of things. Before she went about this work, she should have taken into account whether she was free of hate and vanity, free of the lowly desire to please and feminine coquetry—free of all blame and offense, which she might also have committed, like a sinful Magdalena, in the past. However, it pains me to say: the opposite is still seen in every line of her, in part beautifully written, book; she still appears before us with all those passions, as she tries to portray herself full of beauty and purity, full of love and virtue. Louise should have trusted her *sisters* with a truer feeling for the truth; *we* will never again believe her!

She had consented, I admit with an outburst of immeasurable despair, to give herself to the unloved man. Could she do that? Let no one make us believe that we, even in such extreme cases, need to be "*rape victims*," insofar as we are firm and risk everything rather than become abused. She *had* to suffer for *that* sacrifice of her virginity; no God could save her from that.

We could as easily see the resolution form in the soul of a strong, unspoiled maiden that calls on her to exclaim: "Very well! I *will* not sell my body—run away—better into the arms of want than to the most sensual of all ravishers—sooner to death than to him whom I abhor." I say, just as easily could this resolution form for her as that in which she declares: "I cannot pray—very well then, I will curse. There is no God of love; why else do I suffer. If heaven's mercy is not universal, like rain and sunshine; if it does not also reach me and my pain in blessing here below: then it is nothing but a dream of the fortunate who dress up their sweet privilege in such pretty pictures. I will no longer swear by these dreams. Reality, the reality of this world and her brazen power, has shattered my dreams! All right, I will acknowledge it and fight against it for every square foot of land, which I will transform into a paradise. For the world, which has triumphed over my heart, for the world alone will I live. The money, with which commerce in souls is carried on, to which I sacrificed the ideals of my youth, is indeed the key to the kingdom of this world, to all the sources of pleasure and joy! Money was my doom—it shall remain my doom, which I willingly pursue, against which I no longer foolishly struggle! I vow it solemnly in this agonizing hour and break away from the devout dreams and sacred vows of my youth."

If there is at the beginning of this proclamation a completely reasonable logic against which we can offer no objection, there is, nevertheless, in the despair of the conclusion which immediately follows, something so horrible and shocking that we could despair with her, if we did not have even in the *most wretched* existence another foundation upon which we might still hope someday to base our happiness. That [foundation] is our confidence in ourselves, in our womanly worth, and *often seemingly* only the broken power of that confidence, which must never waver, which we must at least *strive* to hold onto as our final anchor in times of need. I am not even considering the thousands of our sex who are already dead morally and physically; dead even before they could choose the curse or blessing of life and love; nipped in the most fragile bud, even before they blossom in maidenliness; dead and ruined under the protection of privileges which were for sale for gold to a Christian state.

[End of the text of Anneke's essay]

In this early, and perhaps best known, of Anneke's essays, some of the skill and impact of her later essays are already evident. The reader can hear the passion of the later speaker for women's rights in America. Her heavy use of irony to lambaste societal constraints shows all the fervor of a young revolutionary finding her voice. While Anneke is not unaware of or indifferent to the individual facts of the case, especially the impact of divorce on Aston's reputation and finances, she uses Aston's situation because of what it reveals about the circumstances of women in general. She believes that she can count on a certain amount of understanding from her female audience— as well as severe rejection by others who are afraid to challenge the status quo. Because she knows that her ideas will be considered radical in some quarters, she pitches her argument toward the end of the essay to women in their role as mothers and educators of their children. Focusing on the idea of passing on truth to their children, Anneke is able to take the high ground ethically and hopes to avoid the type of criticism leveled at Aston: that she is immoral and indecent. As indicated in the essay, Louise Aston herself wrote about her exile in a pamphlet, *Meine Emancipation, Verweisung und Rechtfertigung* (*My Emancipation, Exile, and Defense*), in which she includes some of the information used by Anneke as the basis for her essay, while adding details about her interview with the authorities and her philosophical point of view.[16] The conflict of the outspoken liberal-minded Aston with the Berlin authorities provided Anneke with an excellent forum for protesting the unequal position of women in nineteenth-century German society.

Notes

1. Joeres presents an intriguing portrait of Aston as an "awkward case," which is ambiguous when examined closely. Aston's public image as a "radical" conflicts with the messages in her writings and with her eventual return to traditional middle-class life in her second marriage. (*Respectability and Deviance* 110–117)

2. The title might be rendered as "Woman in Conflict with Social Relationships," or "Woman in Conflict with Societal Constraints," but a native speaker of English would be much more likely to speak of "conflict with society." The notes added to Anneke's text are mine.

3. This phrase and others in the text are underlined in the original typescript in the Wisconsin Historical Society archives. I have compared this typescript with Mathilde Franziska Anneke's original handwritten manuscript and have retained her emphasis by using italics.

4. Eine jungfräuliche Myrte refers to a bridal wreath.

5. My translation does not capture Anneke's rhyme scheme: aabbccdede. The lines and individual words emphasized in the original appear in italics.

6. The handwritten manuscript in the archives of the Wisconsin Historical Society shows that Anneke may have intended to delete the section beginning with this sentence to the end of the paragraph (i.e., "Since this book's publication…" through "in so many different ways").

7. *Frauenemanzipation im deutschen Vormärz* (82–87) includes excerpts of Anneke's German text in modern script, starting with this sentence, "In her booklet…," and ending after note 12 in this chapter with the sentence: "It's up to you to raise daughters who will never favor a slave with their smile."

8. *Penaten des Hauses* refers to Penates, in Roman mythology "household gods."

9. *Lèse-majesté* is used here to translate the word *Majestätsbeleidigung*, an offense against a sovereign power, in the original text.

10. Anneke plays with the words Vorurtheilen and nachurtheilen to make her point: literally, judging "before" and judging "after."

11. Rudolf von Gottschall (1823–1909), German writer (poetry, fiction, and drama), and early in his career a member of *Junges Deutschland*. The poems mentioned in the essay are written in praise of "free love." Later Gottschall became a political conservative.

12. *Geistig* in German means both "spiritual" and "intellectual," making the choice of one word for the translation often incomplete in comparison to the original text.

13. Epaminondas, c. 418–362 B.C., general and statesman of ancient Thebes (Greece).

14. The Gracchi brothers: Tiberius [Sempronius], 163?–133 B.C., was a Roman reformer and orator; Gaius Sempronius, 153?–121 B.C., was also a political reformer and orator.

15. The typescript identifies the novel as *Aus dem Leben einer Frau* by Louise Aston. Hamburg bei Hoffmann und Campe 1847. It is available in a more modern version: *Aus dem Leben einer Frau: Roman (1847)*. Hrsg. Karlheinz Fingerhut. Stuttgart: H.-D. Heinz Akademischer Verlag, 1982.

16. Two excerpts from Aston's work can be found in *Frauenemanzipation im deutschen Vormärz: Texte und Dokumente*, Renate Möhrmann, ed. (Stuttgart: Reclam, 1978), 66–82.

Chapter 4

Forty-Eighters in Exile (1850–1860)

The price of revolutionary activity for Fritz and Mathilde Anneke was exile, first to Switzerland and then to the United States. In this they joined a group of political refugees who came to be called the "Forty-Eighters."[1] When the Revolution of 1848 failed, they fled to the United States to avoid arrest, imprisonment, and possible execution—as might well have been Fritz Anneke's fate as an officer in the revolutionary army in Baden in 1849. This relatively small group—between 4,000 and 10,000 of the 1,186,000 Germans who arrived in the United States between 1820 and 1860 (Rippley 51)—were generally well educated and idealistic, and wielded great influence through their activism. Rippley describes them as follows:

> Vociferous, strong-headed, often liberal to the point of being radical, the Forty-eighters were refugees from an unsuccessful revolution. As liberals, they were militant critics of America's many religious sects, organized churches, and the established clergy. Intolerant of these new institutions, the Forty-eighters proclaimed their interest in new ideas and were proud to be known as freethinkers. In politics they were violently opposed to slavery and to what they considered corruption in city governments. They opposed fundamentalist religious groups who tried to enact state and local laws for Sunday closing and fought tirelessly against the prohibition of alcoholic beverages. (51–52)

Many Forty-Eighters, including Mathilde Anneke, founded newspapers and gave lectures to spread their ideas. They were considered "outspoken extremists" by many, including more conservative Germans from earlier immigration (Rippley 52).

Mathilde Anneke's achievements are often given special attention (Rippley 56; Hense-Jensen 132–133), and her name was well known during her lifetime, especially as a founder and ardent supporter of the Woman Suffrage Movement. Her voice was raised both for women's rights and against the institution of slavery. Why then is she relatively unknown today? In her 1993 article, Gisela Roethke discusses some of the principal reasons she sees for such neglect. One reason has to do with feminist movements since 1848 constantly "reinventing the wheel" as past accomplishments disappear from the consciousness of current activists; another reason has to do with her work being categorized under German-American immigration, especially in the specialized area of Wisconsin immigration or as a local heroine of Westphalia, which leaves any research on her outside of mainstream research in *Germanistik* (33). However, although Anneke worked closely with such well-known suffragists as Susan B. Anthony and Elizabeth Cady Stanton, and although her contributions are included in *The History of Woman Suffrage* (Stanton, Anthony & Gage), modern history (at least until the 1970s) had a "blind spot" regarding the contributions of women and minorities. Roethke points out that Anneke's greatest contributions involved political activities and journalism within the immigrant German community of the second half of the nineteenth century. Those activities took place in German, and Anneke never really mastered English. In this sense, she was out of the mainstream even in her lifetime. In addition, citing Bus (82ff.), Roethke writes: "with her free-thinking, anti-church, socialistic theories, she [Anneke] swam against the mainstream tendencies of early American feminism, which had held aloft religiously motivated equal rights and temperance as the most important arguments for the improvement of women's lot" (33–34; my translation). The suppression of German language and culture in the United States during World War I made less likely any rediscovery of Anneke's contributions to the Woman Suffrage Movement. In fact, her name is seldom mentioned in current histories of the movement, although where original documents are presented, as with, for example, the Declaration of Rights for Women, July 4, 1876 (see Frost & Cullen-DuPont 399), Anneke's signature appears as testament to her participation.

The women's rights movement in the United States has often been dated from the Seneca Falls Convention of 1848.[2] When Elizabeth Cady Stanton and Lucretia Mott attended the World Antislavery Convention in London during the summer of 1840, it is reported that the seeds of the women's movement were sown when only the men of the U.S. delegation were seated. Allowed to witness the proceedings from the galleries, but not to participate, Stanton and Mott were motivated to consider their own position as women in society. Stanton's isolation as a housewife in Seneca Falls only increased the sense of injustice she had felt in London. When the Motts visited the area, the ensuing conversation between Stanton, Mott, Mrs. Mott's hostess Jane Hunt, Mrs. Mott's sister Martha Wright, and Mary Ann McClintock (Flexner 69) resulted in this momentous Women's Rights Convention, "a convention to discuss the social, civil and religious rights of women," held in the Wesleyan Chapel, Seneca Falls, New York, on July 19–20, 1848.

As Ellen Carol DuBois notes, the development of the women's rights movement in the early years from 1848 to the Civil War had two sources: (1) "women's growing awareness of their common conditions and grievances," and (2) the antislavery movement and the attitudes developed in this era of reform politics (22). Forty-Eighters such as Mathilde Anneke were strong proponents of political reform, and while she is perhaps better known for her role in the Woman Suffrage Movement, her sympathies were also certainly with the Abolition Movement, as was the norm with activist Forty-Eighters.

Like Stanton and Mott, Mathilde Anneke was radicalized as a result of personal experience and contact with reform ideas of her time. Still in Germany in 1848, Anneke had participated in liberal political discussion groups where revolutionary ideas were shared and encouraged. As noted in Chapter 2, she published a newspaper, *Neue Kölnische Zeitung* with her husband, and during his imprisonment she carried on the job alone until the paper was shut down. Her ideas of liberal reform of government, and the inclusion of women in the decision-making process, were radical in mid-nineteenth century Germany, but the atmosphere of reform ideas within her social group stimulated her to examine the position of women in society and to rebel against it. Her best-known essay, "Das Weib im Conflict mit den socialen Verhältnissen" ("Woman in Conflict with Society"), came out of this period in her life.

Anneke's short-lived *Frauen-Zeitung* in Cologne was intended to fight for women's rights, but was suppressed by the censor after two issues. The paper appeared on September 27, 1848, and therefore predates Louise Otto's *Frauenzeitung*, which did not appear until April 1849 (Wagner, *MFA in Selbstzeugnissen* 312). Furthermore, Wagner argues that Anneke is more radical than Otto in that sacrifice and submission are not part of Anneke's view of woman's role. Instead she calls for women to become independent thinkers and agents in their own right. Anneke asks directly: Why after all should women be silent sufferers? Why should they continue to wash the feet of their master as submissive maids? (Wagner, *MFA in Selbstzeugnissen*

313). Women had the ability to influence historical events, in Anneke's
view. In the *Neue Kölnische Zeitung*, she argued that everyone should rebel
against political oppression, and women were not exempt. In fact, women
should stand with the revolutionary men and refuse to have anything to do
with the oppressors (Wagner, *Selbstzeugnisse* 313–314). As discussed previ-
ously, Anneke herself followed her husband into battle, and then into exile
with the fall of Rastatt on July 22, 1849 (Gebhardt 138). Fritz and Mathilde
Anneke became a part of the more than one million refugees in the period
1849–1854 who left Germany in the wake of the failed revolution, and on
October 8, 1849, they and their two children headed for America (Gebhardt
147–149).

Leaving Germany was very difficult for Mathilde Anneke. Writing to her
mother from Zürich on August 15, 1849, she said she did not know what she
would do "in the primeval forests with her only talent that of the pen" (Heinzen manuscript 25). Although she would soon adapt and make her way in
America, her emotions as she went into exile are captured in a poem, repro-
duced in its full length in Regina Ruben's self-published book on Anneke in
1906 (my translation):

In Exile (1849)

You've probably long since forgotten me,
You fortunate ones still at home.
Though I, the banished one, make so bold
As to dream of you continuously.

You shake your head to scold me,
Though once you loved me well,
In return my only penance
Is to love you serenely evermore.

Daily I sneak to your side
And lurk at your garden rails.
Lovingly do I enclose your image
Deeply, ever more deeply in my heart.

Still I hear our belief chided
And [criticism] that I carried our flag

Onward to our encampment,
Onward in our crusade.

I listen still and patient,
As you threaten with malicious words;
Yet I am not so evil and guilty
The flag is still red with blood.

For this flag's beacon
Is love of humanity, and the flood of
Holy blood through which we rushed
Over our dead in the sacred heat of battle.

To freedom, oh, to the only true freedom—
Of which you poor souls do not dream at all,
Which reconciles you and me, scattered troops,
And lovingly unites us in days to come.

Farewell! I need no recompense from you,
Only this: that once you loved me!
My belief, may it reconcile worlds:
My faith grants heaven to everyone.

With such sentiments, Mathilde Anneke leaves the Old World and heads for the New. She is aware from the beginning that she is being torn out of her familiar world with its support network. She is relocating to a situation where she will be, as Dorothea Stuecher so fittingly calls it, "twice removed" from the mainstream of literature. As woman and immigrant, she will face a dual challenge as she tries to earn her living the only way feasible for her— through her writing, both literature and journalism. And she will join others of the German-American community in this disadvantage. As Stuecher writes in the introduction to her book, *Twice Removed: The Experience of German-American Women Writers in the Nineteenth Century*, "This double status acted to twice remove them [the woman writers] from the dominant culture in which they lived and thus influenced their literary status, imprinted their literary imaginations, shaped their professional opportunities and determined their reception in history" (xiii).

The Anneke family, Mathilde, her husband, and two children, left Le-Havre on October 8, 1849 and arrived in New York seven weeks later. They first moved west, intending to build a future with a cousin who lived in Cedarburg, Wisconsin, but by April 3, 1850, they had settled in Milwaukee. The following year Mathilde's mother joined them in Milwaukee with her two unmarried daughters, Johanna and Maria. Fritz Anneke's brother, Carl, also relocated there, and Milwaukee became Mathilde Anneke's real home in America, in spite of several periods of time when she lived elsewhere. In the midwestern German-American community, she would make a name for herself through lectures, newspaper articles, and finally the girls' school she founded in 1865.

Fritz Anneke worked at a series of jobs but was never able to find his niche. Mathilde contributed money she earned through her articles and lectures, although the amount of money tended to be small. An early letter to her mother on December 12, 1850 (from Elgin, Illinois) mentioned Anneke's idea to write a number of "American novels," which she hoped would be of interest in Europe (Wagner, *MFA in Selbstzeugnissen* 82). The subject of money appears often in the letters from this time, as she tried to collect reasonable amounts from publishers for her written work. In the United States, she had little luck getting her book, *Memoiren einer Frau aus dem badisch-pfälzischen Feldzuge* (*Memoirs of a Woman from the Baden-Palatinate Military Campaign*), published, and finally the Annekes self-published the work once they were in Newark, New Jersey, in 1853. Another important project for her was the publication of a new women's newspaper (*Frauen-Zeitung*). In March 1852 the first issue appeared, printed by the editor of the *Volksfreund* (Blackwell 2). Afterward, she accepted the offer of the owner of the *Banner* to print the newspaper, and hired women typesetters to complete the work. This caused immediate protests by the typesetters' union, which blocked the use of women for this task. The power of the union was such that Anneke had to give up the idea of printing her newspaper in Milwaukee.

At this point, the Annekes decided to move back east, hoping for better employment prospects. Before she left, Mathilde completed a lecture tour, which took her to Detroit, Cleveland, Buffalo, Boston, Pittsburgh, Philadelphia, and New York, as well as several other destinations (Wagner, *MFA in Selbstzeugnissen* 76). The tour was very successful, both with the size of audiences and in a financial sense. The children stayed temporarily in Milwaukee with Mathilde's mother, and Fritz set out for Newark where he purchased a small printing press, made possible by the funds earned by

Mathilde's lecture tour. During the period from 1850 to 1860, both Annekes were very active in journalism, writing many articles for the German-American press, and editing their own newspapers. The *Newarker Zeitung*, founded in February 1853, became Newark's first German-language daily newspaper, and the press also made it possible for Mathilde to publish her own *Deutsche Frauen-Zeitung*, the "first journal in America founded to promote women's rights" (Blackwell 3). It is historically important as the first feminist newspaper published independently by a woman in the United States (Wagner, *MFA in Selbstzeugnissen* 315). The *Deutsche Frauen-Zeitung* appeared from 1852 to1854, first monthly and then later bimonthly, and finally weekly in Milwaukee, New York, and Newark, and reached a substantial number of subscribers (Roethke 42), despite criticism of Anneke's radical ideas, and the opposition of men. Anneke refers to a quasi "conspiracy" of husbands against the paper. Asked for the reason for their opposition, she notes their answer: "Meine Frau ist aufgeklärt genug, es ist nicht nötig, daß dieselbe noch mehr aufgeklärt werde" ("My wife is enlightened enough; it is not necessary for her to become any more enlightened.") (Wagner, *MFA in Selbstzeugnissen* 317).

The one extant issue, from October 15, 1852, shows Anneke's intention to rouse women to action for their own emancipation. Included in this issue are a feminist ballad presented in both German and English ("Eine alltägliche Geschichte"/ "An Everyday Tale"), in which the unmarried mother is forced by economic circumstances to become a prostitute, and parts of a provocative speech by Ernestine Rose from October 19, 1851, in Boston (Wagner, *MFA in Selbstzeugnissen* 321). In her introduction to the text, Anneke praises Ernestine Rose for her radical thinking and cites her courage in standing up to the "bitterest enemies of all freedom and independence, the bitterest enemies of all striving for happiness" (her German text reads: "die bittersten Feinde aller Freiheit und Unabhängigkeit, die bittersten Feinde allen Glückseligkeitsstrebens"), namely religion, the priesthood, and the Bible (Roethke 44; Wagner 321). In an article (a letter from Boston) about the opening of the New England Drawing School for Women, the radical idea of giving women the opportunity to pursue education for a profession was stressed. Considering such articles, and in later editions, selections from Hippel, Mary Wollstonecraft, Margaret Fuller, and others, as well as a reprint of her own essay "Das Weib im Conflict mit den socialen Verhältnissen" (according to a letter written by Anneke to Alexander Jonas; Wagner, *MFA in Selbstzeugnissen*

322), the newspaper was amazingly successful in the face of the generally conservative nature of the German immigrant community.

For six years, life in Newark was good to the Annekes. Family life went well, and the Annekes supported each other's professional efforts. The *Newarker Zeitung* supported a comfortable lifestyle, including some acreage in the Philadelphia area. However, before the smallpox epidemic of 1858, two of the Anneke children died in Newark, one shortly after birth, and one at age three; and during the epidemic, the whole family fell ill with smallpox, and the older boy Fritz (ten at the time), as well as two-year-old twin, Irla, died. From the letters Mathilde wrote to her mother, it is easy to read what a horrible blow this was to her. She had lost four of the six children she and Fritz had together, and she never fully recovered from their deaths. The immediate result was their decision to sell the press and return to Milwaukee. However, the close family life enjoyed by the Annekes in Newark was lost once they made that move. During the rest of their lives, there were long periods during which Fritz and Mathilde no longer lived together. In fact, about a year after their arrival in Milwaukee, in May 1859, Fritz Anneke departed for Italy where he hoped to serve as newspaper correspondent, covering the renewed uprising there. Mathilde Anneke remained behind with the children.

When the Annekes first returned to Milwaukee, they developed a friendship with abolitionist Sherman Booth and his wife, Mary. They even stayed with them when their own house was flooded (Blackwell 3). Mathilde and Mary Booth became close friends and supported each other through many difficulties. She writes in a letter to Fritz in September 1859 that since she has found someone dear in the United States, she no longer feels like she is in exile; she even feels as if she is at home ("Ich fühle jetzt Heimatluft hier wehen"; Wagner, *MFA in Selbstzeugnissen* 112). Mary's marriage was in trouble, and she was considering a divorce at the time when Sherman was jailed for helping a slave escape. Fritz Anneke's letters from Europe, meanwhile, persuaded Mathilde to consider traveling there to join him. In a letter from August 1859, she wrote: "How pleasant the stay in Zurich must be for you. How often have I thought about that beautiful country. Sometimes it seems to me as if I feel homesick for the blue lake" (Wagner, *MFA in Selbstzeugnissen* 107). That thought seems to have stayed with her, and her feelings of nostalgia finally caused her to decide to take on the long trip. She did not have to abandon her newfound friendship because of this decision, as Mary Booth decided to accompany her. In July 1860 the two women, along with Mathilde's children Percy and Hertha, and Mary's daughter Lilian headed for Zurich, arriving first in Bremen on August 19. After a visit in Dortmund, they finally arrived in Zurich on August 27 (Wagner, *MFA in Selbstzeugnissen* 131).

During the period before leaving Milwaukee, Mathilde Anneke remained very active in journalism, in particular writing theater and music critiques. Wagner also cites in the *Selbstzeugnissen* a number of longer articles for the *Belletristische Zeitung* about important women including Margaret Fuller, Mary Wollstonecraft, and Louise Aston. Parts of her earlier essay "Das Weib im Conflict mit den socialen Verhältnissen" ("Woman in Conflict with Society") also appeared in print (127–128). Along with her newspaper correspondence, she talks of working on a novel, and she describes an active cultural life with like minded people. This was a very productive period in her professional life.

Mathilde Anneke had clearly hoped to reunite the family in Switzerland, but she was to be disappointed. After a year of relative ease and happy family life, during which the Annekes quickly reestablished old contacts with the European press, the U.S. Civil War broke out. In September 1861, having gathered the necessary funds, Fritz Anneke returned to the United States to join the Union Army, while Mathilde and Mary Booth remained in Switzerland. They did not return to Milwaukee until 1865 with the end of the war, in spite of much financial hardship. Neither Sherman Booth, who had gone bankrupt, nor Fritz Anneke, whose career in the Union Army ended with his discharge, was able to provide much financial support. However, this "Swiss Period" of her career, from 1860 to 1865, turned out to be the most productive literary period of Mathilde Anneke's life. She wrote a very large number of newspaper reports and background articles on the Civil War, and in addition her most important stories and novels (Wagner, *MFA in Selbstzeugnissen* 131). She also met the family of Professor Kapp, whose daughter Cäcilie would later move back to Milwaukee with Mathilde and found a school for girls, the *Milwaukee Töchterinstitut*, with her.

As mentioned before, Mathilde Anneke shared the difficulties inherent in being an immigrant writer. This placed her at the periphery of American culture to start with, and in addition, being a woman trying to pursue a public career, she faced a conservative community not particularly supportive of women's literary production. As Stuecher points out, the period 1850–1890 was characterized by the entrance of women writers into the popular novel market, both in Germany and in the United States (23). She mentions novelists Eugenie Marlitt, Ida Hahn-Hahn, Fanny Lewald, Louise Otto, Louise

Mühlbach, and Marie von Ebner-Eschenbach, who were also popular with the German-American public. In the United States, the same phenomenon of women novelists was also occurring, including in their numbers the well-known Harriet Beecher Stowe. However, immigrant life seems to have isolated German-American women writers and impacted their self-confidence and professional activity, limiting the number who were able to pursue paid literary activities. Interestingly, poetry appeared more frequently, as it "was 'manageable' in its time requirements, and it was a form which at once seemed 'cultured' and 'feminine' to the immigrant community. Added to this was the reality that it was seldom remunerated by the press and thus could become 'public' without assuming the high profile of a 'professional' writer" (Stuecher 26). As a political activist, Mathilde Anneke wrote newspaper articles when she first arrived and dealt with the daily challenges of raising a family amid financial difficulties. As an immigrant, she did not feel fully at home in either Anglo- or German-American societies. Her major literary work after her immigration occurred when she returned to Switzerland, the first stop on her exile from Germany. She and Fritz Anneke were able to step back into a familiar society and make the connections they had once had with the European press. Although changed by her American experiences, she seems to have found Switzerland psychologically comfortable and supportive of her literary efforts. Once she returned to Milwaukee, she returned to writing articles, this time about European current events, which were of great interest to the immigrant population (Stuecher 35).

Most of Mathilde Anneke's literary work during this time shows that she is clearly part of the *Vormärz*. Her stories carry within them an ideological conflict, focused particularly on the antislavery question and the parallel implications she sees for women's rights. One exception is her short work, "Als der Grossvater die Grossmutter nahm" ("When Grandfather Married Grandmother"), a sort of family memoir and written tribute to the place of her birth. Both "Die Sclaven-Auction" ("Slave Auction"), which appeared in *Didaskalia* in June 1862, and "Gebrochene Ketten" ("Broken Chains"), which appeared in the *Milwaukee Herald* in June 1864 and again in *Der Bund* in November 1864, are strong indictments of slavery. Anneke incorporates her friend, abolitionist Gerrit Smith, from whom she received frequent letters while in Switzerland, into her story "Sclaven-Auction" (Wagner, *MFA in Selbstzeugnissen* 169–170; a letter to her mother of September 25, 1862, mentions the letters and later mentions her work on the short story). Both stories are set in the South, with the intention of revealing the horrors of slavery by showing the personal human costs, including the auction itself, the separation of families, and the despair of a slave mother who kills her own child to keep it from enduring a life of slavery. Anneke's focus in these stories is the plight of women, who are doubly exploited as women and as slaves. And her fictional, symbolic solution to the oppression of these female characters is to have them freed, as she does Lelia in "Gebrochene Ketten" and Isabella in "Sclaven-Auction" (Stuecher 72).

The novel *Das Geisterhaus in New York* (1864) (*Haunted House in New York*) is Anneke's translation of an anonymous serial novel. However, when the ending was not available to her, she was forced to write the final chapters herself. In a letter from November 3, 1861 (Wagner, *MFA in Selbstzeugnissen* 152), she refers to her "brilliantly finished *Geisterhaus*" ("brilliant beendetes *Geisterhaus*"); so she must have been satisfied with the way she completed it. Her ending is full of pathos, and as emotionally dramatic as an Italian opera: a throng of mourners in procession follow the caskets of the Italian immigrant mother and child to their graves (Struecher 70). With this gesture, society shows a concern for these immigrants in death, which it did not seem to demonstrate while they were alive. Stuecher sees in Anneke's immigrant fiction optimism about the possibility of cultural pluralism and the acceptance of immigrants into the dominant culture. Perhaps her best expression of this is the novella, "Uhland in Texas," which appeared in the *Illinois Staatszeitung* in April 1866. The German immigrants to Texas are warmly welcomed, and they live in a type of utopia on their plantation "Uhland." Anneke's fictional Wallenstein is the embodiment of an ideal Forty-Eighter, an intelligent humanist who could fit in with his new American environment. In this, Mathilde Anneke was idealizing, rather than reflecting, her own experience and that of her husband. Settled in the West, the German-Americans drew together in times of danger and were able to handle the violence of Indian attacks and of the Civil War with skill and courage. Interestingly, the idealized women of the story are independent American women—although by making Indianna a woman of both German (assimilated German-American immigrant) and Native American blood, she is in essence creating a new synthesis. As Stuecher notes: "Just as Anneke had eliminated the insecurity and alienation from the immigrant experience, she also retired the German immigrant heroine…. To stand on equal footing with men, Anneke's women needed verve and forthrightness, characteristics which were antithetical to the quiet resignation and noble enduring which had characterized the former idealization of German womanhood" (77). When German women did appear in her fiction, Anneke created them as unsuited to the new vigorous world of active social change, destined for helplessness and an early death.

Overall, Mathilde Anneke did not have great success in her literary efforts. Her lectures and newspaper articles capture the force and tenor of her ideas and arguments, and while some of that same vigor can be seen in the fiction, along with the emotional pathos so frequent in nineteenth-century fiction, interest in her work all but disappeared after her death. Indeed, even during her lifetime, the ambivalence of the immigrant community toward a woman of such strong convictions played a role in denying her any great success. As Stuecher describes it (44): "Mathilde Anneke, the heroine of the 1848 revolution, was a figure which the immigrant community could pay respect to and elevate to notoriety. But Anneke the immigrant, who feigned no indifference to success and who spoke up for women's rights at Anglo American women's rights rallies, experienced rejection by the German-American community." The conflict between her own radical ideas and the conservative German-American community may well have undermined her confidence, and seems to have contributed to her abandonment of her novel *Der Sturmgeiger* (the title refers to a Westphalian musician) after ten chapters. Although she worked on it during the period 1862–1865, and according to a letter written to Fritz Anneke in November 1861 (Wagner, *MFA in Selbstzeugnissen* 152), she had hoped to finish it that winter if all went well, it remained unpublished. The demands and obstacles of immigrant life, which she and her husband also experienced as they tried to make their way in America and find appropriate work that would pay the bills, conflicted with her need to be creative and express her ideas. Under such circumstances, the indifference of readers and the reluctance of publishers to pay for work must have made it difficult to continue.

One major source of strength and support throughout Mathilde Anneke's life seems to have been her women friends and family. Her writings show she did not devalue women or their contributions to society, and she always believed in their ability to influence society. Perhaps her first role model was her mother, who was an important part of Anneke's life in Germany and also later in the United States when her mother immigrated and settled in Milwaukee. She also had a close mentoring relationship with Cäcilie Kapp with whom she founded her school, which will be discussed in the chapter in this book on education for women. In Switzerland, Mary Booth's friendship and collaboration on literary works was a source of comfort and professional stimulus during her Civil War years as a correspondent in Europe. In a letter to Fritz Anneke on August 2, 1863, Anneke wrote that she and Mary planned to work together on a volume of American short stories under the title *Gebrochene Ketten*. Anneke admired Mary's inventive ideas, but noted that she [Anneke] was better able to put those ideas in writing (Wagner, *MFA in Selbstzeugnissen* 180). This plan was not realized, however, before Mary returned to the United States in July 1864 due to illness, and died a year later. Anneke's deeply moving poem, "Entblättert" ("The Leaves Have Fallen"), dedicated to Mary Booth, reflects the depth of her loss (Ruben 22).

Finally, the first woman in the United States to have a major impact on Anneke's future was Ernestine Rose. Anneke's admiration for her was clear, as can be seen by Anneke's introduction to selections from a speech by Rose printed in her *Frauen-Zeitung*. At her first appearance before a Women's Rights Conference in New York City in 1853, Ernestine Rose served as her interpreter. Both women were immigrants and therefore had the basis of that common experience, and they both became major figures in the Woman Suffrage Movement, espousing bold ideas considered radical by society. This struggle to change the position of women in society was also the basis for admiration of, and friendship with, major figures in the Suffrage Movement such as Elizabeth Cady Stanton and Susan B. Anthony. Mathilde Anneke's dedication to this struggle formed an integral part of her activism in America before she left for Switzerland, and she continued her work for the Movement upon her return to the United States in 1865.

Notes

1. As Maria Wagner, among others, has noted, the term "Forty-Eighter" is used two different ways: One, to refer to all the immigrants who came to the United States around the middle of the nineteenth century, the majority of whom came for economic reasons, and two, to refer to political refugees who fled into exile, hoping to enjoy freedom in the United States (*MFA in Selbstzeugnissen* 73). The Annekes are Forty-Eighters in both senses, but I focus on their situation as political refugees. (In regard to spelling, I use "Forty-Eighters" except in direct quotes where the author uses "Forty-eighters.")

2. Nancy Isenberg discusses "competing accounts of the events leading to the Seneca Falls Convention" in Chapter 1 of her book, *Sex and Citizenship in Antebellum America*. See especially pages 4–6.

Chapter 5

A Sketch from American Life

During her stay in Switzerland during the U.S. Civil War (1860–1865), Mathilde Franziska Anneke was very productive in her writing. Clearly the conflicts of the Civil War impressed her, and she wrote many newspaper articles and reports to explain the issues and events to her European readers. As an exile in Switzerland, she also had the distance and objectivity to reflect on her U.S. experience. Before discussing Anneke's contributions to the struggle for women's rights in the United States, which spanned time periods both before and after her years in Switzerland, let us examine one of her essays in the form of a travelogue, which will serve to illustrate an important strength in her writing of the period. She had the ability to capture a scene or situation in a relatively brief descriptive narration, which also revealed her attitude about current social issues, in this case, her position on slavery and her concern about the treatment of Native Americans. Excerpts from a little-known article, entitled "Erinnerungen vom Michigan-See" ("Memories of Lake Michigan"), for the *Elberfelder Zeitung* shows her skill in this type of reporting.[1]

Memories of Lake Michigan

The "Iowa," one of the most powerful and most elegant propeller-driven ships that plow the blue waters of Lake Michigan, planned to leave the harbor of Milwaukee on July 21 at noon.

We planned to say farewell to a friend, who, for his humane deed of rescuing a slave from the hands of his persecutor, was held as a prisoner behind iron doors in the cold marble fortress[2] by the slavery-supporting government, and whom we had tried for weeks in vain to free by force. We couldn't reach him until twelve and so it was quite clear that we would not be able to depart until around one.

Captain Jones, a kind man who was quite anxious to have the pleasure of our company during the long trip on the open lake, decided under the circumstances to delay his departure until one.

Our farewell was short, but with double the sorrow that accompanies a usual separation. A handshake—a tear in which the hope of a quick release was mirrored, and a radiant gleam in the eye, which declared thanks in the name of freedom—then a farewell, until we meet again!

The constables of the slaveholding power unbolted the doors; the guards led us up the great iron stairs and let us out for the last time.

From the window of the United States prison-fortress, the prisoner could look out over the wide blue lake; it was a "tower on the beach" in which he languished and suffered, a victim of savagery and barbarism in the land of freedom and independence.

A carriage brought us quickly to the harbor, where the proud "Iowa" awaited us with billowing smokestacks. Captain Jones received us with the courtesy of an old seaman of the upper lakes and helped us to cross the moveable bridge from land to the ship.

In the large room of this swimming palace was all the comfort and luxury that Americans of the Northwest are accustomed to keep around them. Our berths were roomy and elegant, the beds inviting and shimmering in white linen coverlets and white angora bedspreads.

Immediately after our arrival on board the captain gave the order to depart, and after several wide, majestic turns we had the brilliant panorama of the shining white city, the queen of the northwest,[3] spread out before our eyes.

From the proud fortress, the triumphant Stars and Stripes fluttered, and near her from a small window opening, the white cloth in the chained hands of our imprisoned friend waved to and fro.

Indeed, a plaintive parody of that proud freedom poem, which once toned as victoriously as the sound of the music of the spheres. Many stars have become dull and silent, and the harmony of the anthem lost amid the clanking of slave chains.

With great haste, the keel of our proud steamship cut through the high billowing flood of old Michigan, and, almost reaching the high seas, we had once again the full view of the beautiful hill city which, in her characteristic marble whiteness and in the brightness of the sun, shone far and wide in every direction. You can boldly travel through a large part of the North American states in any direction, south and east, but you will find no other city which offers a more charming and at the same time imposing view than Milwaukee.

Scarcely forty years have rolled by since the first white man directed his footsteps to this hilly shore and hesitantly set his foot in the small Indian village, where the gleaming "white stone city" [4] now spreads out [in front of us]. At that time, when the red men still lived here, they named the place "Manawoukie." This name derives from a root used by the Indians for medicinal purposes because they trusted its great healing power, and not found in any other place in the area. This root was called manwau, and the combination of syllables Ma-na-wan-kie in the Indian language has no other meaning than "rich land of the Manwu." The Indians described this plant as a root that grew nowhere else as far as they knew. This root was revered by them for being very powerful, and the Chippewas on Lake Superior used to give a whole beaver fur for one piece of this only as big as a man's finger. It was not an actual medicine, but rather a beautiful aroma, which they mixed into almost all of the medicine they ingested.

[In the next paragraphs, Anneke interjects an account of the founding of Milwaukee by a French fur trader named Salomon Juneau and an Indian woman, which would have been of interest to her European audience because of the particular interest of the time in anything "exotic," or from the American West. Anneke's admiration of this man and his good relations with the chief of the local tribe, as well as her admiration for his wife, portrayed in the report as rejecting anything that would present her with "too great a contradiction with her natural habits and the customs of her forest," is evident in the description of their life. The pair had many children, and the wife became known for her care of the sick whatever their race. Both were greatly mourned at their death, and Juneau was deeply honored as someone "sent by the Great Spirit" and even more revered than the president of the United States. A town and a county of the state of Wisconsin were named after him. In several paragraphs Anneke details the funeral customs followed by the Indians in this case, including the special anniversary remembrances. After this interlude she continues with her description of their journey.]

Little by little Milwaukee disappeared from sight, and soon the southern point of land which reached far into our small lake could also no longer be seen. The sun was already low in the west, and the sky glimmered like emerald and gold. The lake was rather quiet and looked more and more blue so that the white sails of our small skipping vessel stood out from the wonderful tinted background waves like a blinding field of snow. It was hard to pull oneself away from this magical sight, but it was necessary, and we moved from the deck into the salon.

The people had already gathered there and evidently were waiting for the sound of the gong that would invite them to the dinner table.

The captain appeared; the steward tapped the dinner-gong, an instrument which sounded very musical to many ears, and as if driven by steam power, the agile kitchen servants hurried forth with their laden silver platters. The elderly ship's monarch took his seat at the head of the table, with Owaissa on his right side and me on the left near him. He was very talkative and in a good mood, in spite of the fact that the latest storms upon his entrance into the harbor had cost him sleepless nights. He was of the opinion that an old Jack Tar sailor like himself no longer needed much sleep; he had enough with four hours rest out of twenty-four. The voyage over the northern lakes, however, required great watchfulness if we did not want to lose our way, tangle with daring pirate schooners, or get stranded on [one of] the hundred small islands. The inhabitants of these islands, the old redskins,[5] were, according to him, friendly enough to visitors to take into their wigwams anyone stranded there, but it was better and more prudent to have only short visits with them near the landing sites than to be forced to make a longer stay. He remarked that we had chosen a favorable time for our excursion, and that we would have an opportunity, not only to meet with Indians at the landings on several islands, but also to encounter several older chieftains on their boats, who, because of the annual payment to the Indians by the United States in La Pointe, would be making their way there, frequently by boat.

Our dinner table was not yet cleared when the call came that we were arriving in Port Washington. A chieftain—or only a simple red man—a squaw—a papoose[6] —or any kind of living being from the wilderness was certainly part of our expectations. So we hurried out on deck and glimpsed the small friendly village with her harbor before us, but not a trace of a redskin.

[During their short stay in port, a few people got on. Although the narrator expresses disappointment at not seeing any Native Americans, a young man boards the ship, a man who Owaissa says has something "noteworthy" about him. As the ship leaves the harbor, gliding on Lake Michigan "almost like a graceful gondola," all head to their berths. In the second section of the report, we discover that a Winnebaga chieftain named A-haw-mongha has come on board. The visitors see him for the first time looking intently at the glass chandeliers in the salon.]

When we came out of our berths the next day, we were greeted by our old captain with a smile on his face. He had an event to share with us, which he was sure would be of interest, namely that, on a small island, which we had passed in the night and whose name was illegible in my memo-book, he had taken on board the Winnebaga chieftain A-haw-mongha. This man planned to head to Minkepink, one of the Manitou islands, to visit some friendly tribes.

When I turned around, I got a good look at him, deep in contemplation of the glass chandelier in the salon. A bright fresh ray of morning light streamed through the colored pieces and played around the prism-formed glass which decorated the chandelier.

The face of the chieftain, whose features were noble, even admirable, at that moment took on the expression of increasing amazement. And suddenly, as if gripped by an extraordinary desire, he sprang with a single leap to the captain, grabbed his hand, pulled him nearer into position, and pointed to the crystals which looked like jewels in the colors of the universe. Then suddenly with a haste that almost startled us, he tore off his waistband and other war ornaments, laid them at the feet of the captain with an indescribable expression, and pleaded for him to take all of that in exchange for this "light from the Great Spirit."

The captain did not understand him, or the old, rough seaman didn't want to understand him, I don't know which. It was enough that Owaissa, for whom the Indian language in its heartfelt references was not at all strange, went up to him, [took] his hand, and said with an expression with which she could have vouched for heaven itself: "Oh, certainly, most certainly! You shall have it."

In the meantime several of the ship's company had entered the salon, including the young man, who on the previous evening had been observed by Owaissa as a not-at-all-uninteresting figure. Silent and indifferent, he headed even today to the loneliest corners of the ship and found himself at the opposite side of the room where this scene was taking place. However, when he noticed the great commotion there, he turned around. His attention was undoubtedly even more alert when he saw the Indian as the group's center of attention. He quickly walked up to him, spoke to him in a melodious manner of speech, which I can only assume was an Indian language, scarcely waited for the man's answer before turning immediately to the captain with a more severe and then pleading expression, and spoke in fluent English: "Trade with our red brother for one of these crystals, which distributes the light of the Great Spirit."

In the friendliest manner, the captain himself climbed up on the table, above which the chandelier hung, loosened a wire on which the small crystal rod was fastened, and handed the piece to Owaissa. She reached immediately for the "magic pouch" of the Indian, which, with all its marvelous treasures, he had placed at the feet of the captain as the possessor of the "light of the Great Spirit" which seemed to him so valuable. She placed the cut glass with the rest of the "priceless" objects and carefully fastened the waistband on which the pouch was attached around him again.

Without saying a word and with a truly classic calmness, which revealed itself quite suddenly in the behavior of the Indian, he carried his pouch containing the precious treasure away from there. Only now and then did he return, seemingly with the same equanimity, however looking intently at Owaissa, whom he must have taken for a beautiful angel. Occasionally he would approach her and confidentially stroke her forehead and her beautiful eyebrows with his hand and call her the intermediary between him and the Great Spirit.

Everything the Indian said would have remained an eternal riddle to us poor pale faces, if the young stranger had not been so kind as to translate the melodious Indian sounds into English.

But who was this man who understood it?

He was one of the few people we encountered on the civilized routes of America who still spoke and understood the sounds of the red men, which will soon die away completely. He was a real average pale face, and where, in heaven's name, did he learn the language of the forest?

We got after our old friend, the captain, to search out the secret; from him we hoped to obtain accurate information about the stranger who had now become very interesting to me. Mr. Jones, however, did not want to draw him out in conversation. Maybe he was not particularly fond of chatting, or maybe we were passing some reefs and shoals which demanded his full attention and skill as a seaman? Well, this much we found out from him about the stranger: he was traveling in the area of the upper lake, perhaps even stopping in La Pointe in order to serve as a translator in the negotiations between the Chippewa tribes who attended and the United States Commission.

A living Indian Chronicle, which we stumbled upon here by coincidence! An Indian Chronicle, and not even in hieroglyphics, no, in writing legible to us. But how to open up that remarkable book which could contain so many interesting things for us! Perhaps only Owaissa understood how to solve that problem.

Indeed, the stranger was like a closed book with seven seals! A quiet earnestness, which seemed to indicate a deep melancholy, lay on his pale features. His soft dark hair, which fell in curls around the fine shape of his head, his refined demeanor, and the sudden surge of liveliness which, although innate, seemed held back in life by certain restraints, led me to deduce a good parentage, perhaps of French origin.

[The day passes, and as evening arrives people begin to gather together.]

Owaissa took advantage of the first good opportunity to speak with our tall stranger. In their mutual sympathies, and to a greater or lesser degree also in their relations with the red race, these two people obviously shared a common interest. That Owaissa carried in her veins the blood of a European ancestor was evident without a letter of introduction[7] as her proof; the foreigner, at least, had seen that about her at first sight.

"You take an interest in the natives of our country," she said to him. "You understand their language and can be very useful to our poor Indian brothers. Have you learned their different dialects?"

"The Chippewa language is more or less my mother tongue," he replied somewhat hesitantly.

"But you are not of Indian descent?" she objected in a questioning tone.

"The beginning of my life I know nothing about—not even about my father and mother," was the answer.

"Don't you know anything about your poor mother?" she asked more urgently.

"Nothing at all! An elderly, loyal, motherly redskin raised me. She divulged to me that Eagle, a feared chieftain of the time, stole me along with the silk coverlet of my first cradle. The elderly squaw, O-kee-wah was her name, taught me first to babble in her language. The first memories of my childhood are connected to her and to my blue-velvet outfit, which by all appearances belonged to another sphere than that of the forest."

"And you have no memories of your mother?"

"None," he answered agitated. "But when I think of her, it is as if a shadow passes over my eyes."

There followed a deep pause; the moon threw a blinding ray on the still waves of the lake and before his teary eyes arose the image of a heavenly vision from the depths.

In the wigwam of his Indian friends, near the fires of the warriors, the little white boy played until he was around five or six. Then he was forced to exchange his red foster mother for a white mother. The matter was handled simply. One day his tribe was on an excursion and he followed. Having arrived in the streets of a city, the wife of the elderly Commodore Grinon met them, and her attention was strongly drawn to the loveable white boy. All the feelings of her motherly heart were awakened, and she did not give up pleading for the boy. Her elderly, equally humane husband, went to the Indians, found the owners, and gave them a hundred dollars for the little Che-ma-ka-mun.[8]

The little stranger soon became the darling of the old Commodore and his noble wife; however, when after a number of years they died, he returned to his red friends. He mastered their language and several different dialects of other tribes, [and] learned their customs and habits, as well as their history insofar as it could be read from the runic inscriptions on their few monuments or in their traditions.

So he lived with the ample means his elderly foster father had generously provided for him, alternating between wigwams and the cities of civilization. He was a mediator in the negotiations between the United States and the red men in regard to their hunting grounds, and a faithful representative of the interests of the latter. On their paydays he stood at their side as advisor and spokesman. That is why he found himself en route now to La Pointe where the payments to the Chippewa were again to take place. We pressed him for some information about his experiences, and he did not hesitate to tell us in several discussions about interesting occurrences from the previous years which he witnessed, and to permit me to copy down documents which he took from his satchel.

[In the third and last part of her essay, Anneke reports one of the young man's experiences during the annual payment to the Chippewa Indians by the United States government, which was scheduled to take place in August and September 1855. Agents from the Department of Indian Affairs arrived, but the meeting had to be delayed because the Indians were not yet there. Although the government had ordered it, no message had been sent to them informing them of the time and place selected for their annual meeting. Because of this glitch in communications, the agents had to send messages to the outlying tribes. Meanwhile the near-by tribes arrived just as they always had out of habit. There was a period of waiting and joking while everyone waited. I pick up the story at this point.]

It was a bright, cheerful day. The sun stood high in the sky at midday when the small vessels sent to bring the children of the forest across finally arrived. These boats were heavily laden with men, women, and children, and plowed through the surging waters with a rim of scarcely the breadth of a hand. Everyone crowded toward the shore to see the newcomers.

But what poverty, what suffering stared us in the face…. Instead of being wrapped in blankets, their little ones were mostly naked or wrapped in rags. Rough, untanned deer hides and hides from other animals were the only covering for the men and women. The whole supply of the trade goods they brought with them consisted of birch-bark baskets.

Weak from hunger and sickness, some of these once so powerful sons of the wilderness had to drag themselves along, leaning on the arms of their brothers. A great number were lame and blind. For a long time they had lived on nothing but wild rice; they could neither hunt nor fish because they had to flee with their sick and with the children so as not to fall into an ambush of their enemies. The previous year they also showed up very late for payment, and, since most of the wares had already been distributed, they left very empty-handed.

Na-naw-ong-ga-be was the chieftain of this unfortunate tribe; their hunting grounds lay between thirty and sixty miles from the Mississippi. The land of their irreconcilable enemies, the blood-thirsty Sioux, lay on the other side. Their deadly feuds and wars of extermination have lasted for centuries, and every means, all attempts of their white neighbors and of the United States government itself, to settle the disputes have been fruitless.

Everyone had to admit that the warriors of this tribe distinguished themselves above all the others in La Pointe by their noble features and fine, upright stature. Their intellectual strength also seemed excellent and not yet broken down. Their highest chieftain, Na-naw-ong-ga-be, was one of the first speakers on the site.

Not long after their arrival, the commissioner sent this request to them: "the tribe should gather to receive the payment of the United States." Within two to three hours, one hundred stately warriors led by Na-naw-ong-ga-be appeared before the United States official. They marched before him, one after the other in regular file, like those who are accustomed to go on the warpath. Their highest chieftain, I think I can say, had seen more than fifty-five winters. He is not exceptionally tall, but of a noble, strong stature; his intelligent face carries a wild expression; his sharp eyes, flashing as he speaks, brighten with a proud and sparkling shine. Like most of the warriors, his face is colored in purple. When leading his warriors and in councils, he wears a headdress of turkey feathers which flows over his head and shoulders and gives a majestic and wild appearance to his person.

Very soon after his arrival, this chieftain had become the favorite spokesman around whom everyone crowded. Our narrator, who was continually present during these memorable days in La Pointe, was full of praise for him, and carried the memory of him and his people, like all the interesting moments of his life, faithfully in his heart, and noted down the speeches of the red man in his journal. He is convinced that this tribe of Indians has inborn in them as noble impulses as could live in any human heart. He said that when he landed in La Pointe, he saw many of those present crying tears of empathy and of the deepest compassion, upon seeing the wretched procession of this tribe of people.

The line of warriors placed themselves in a circle; at Na-naw-ong-ga-be's side sat Aw-ke-wain-ze, another chieftain of slim build and majestic carriage, who was taller by a head than the warriors sitting around him. His tomahawk rested at his side, and the pipe was handed around.

Johnson von dem Soo served as translator. He was half Chippewa and a man of intelligence and outstanding character. His place was in the middle of the circle of his red brothers.

The commissioner started the conversation and began by speaking to the chieftain: he was delighted to see him and his people, although they had come very late: he felt painfully touched to see them in such a sad situation and so beaten down by poverty.

Na-naw-ong-ga-be responded in an earnest and worthy manner: "My father, we are also very happy to see you. We had reasons why we did not come immediately, when we heard your voice echo through the wilderness. Your voice excited happy feelings and joy among all my tribe. I lost no time in giving orders that all my young people should assemble around me. However, I had second thoughts that it was not advisable to break camp at once because we were all busy collecting wild rice to ensure that my people would not suffer from hunger and want. I urged them to hurry to take care of our old and sick women as well as our children. I also left four of my best warriors behind to defend everyone from the dangerous, warlike Sioux. But then I and my people hurried over the trails to the wide shores of the Chippewa Lake (they call Lake Superior by that name). I obeyed your command and am now with you.

You say, my father, you are grieved to see us in our pitiable condition. It is no wonder, my father, that you see us in misery, and that we show you our nakedness. Five long winters have passed since I have received so much as a single blanket for one of my children.

My father, what has become of the promise you gave us? I believe you have sent us what you promised, but where has it arrived? That is more than I can tell you. Maybe it sank in the deep waters of the lake, or it has gone into the air as smoke like the rising fog, or flew over our heads and into the setting sun? Last year I visited our father (he meant the Indian agent Mr. Gilbert), who came here and distributed wares to his red children—however I could not come at that time—and received nothing. I turned to our traders one after the other—undoubtedly they are standing here behind us—and asked them to give me some clothing for my poor children, but they turned me away. So I had to set my feet on the long way home and return to my homeland forests with empty hands just as I had come.

In your words to me, you have always admonished me not to use firewater. When the traders refused me, as I told you, I had decided not to accept any firewater if they should offer it to me.

I returned home. With what nature had provided for us, we withstood a long cold winter. We relied on only the pelts we took from the animals of the forest. I could only sit by my small fire for lack of the things which I had not received from my father, and which I could not get from the traders. I begged my father to bring me next year what I so very much needed. I am not like your red children who live near the shores of the Chippewa Lake—and who demand that you bring them iron for fish spears and twine to sink the hooks in the water. I tell you, my father, I live mainly by going through my homeland forests with a weapon on my shoulder, and when I follow a wild animal, it falls before me. I have come with my young people, and we have brought many from our family along because of your promise from previous years so that you might give us a good portion of our present-year needs. And like all your children, my father, I am hungry after a long day's work or a long trek; my people need something to give them strength. It has been a long time since we were given firearms. We now only have some clubs bundled together with leather bands to kill our prey and to defend ourselves against our enemies.

My father, look around at the faces of my poor people; sickness and hunger, firewater and war are killing us quickly. We are dying and withering away; we fall on the ground like trees before the skill of the white man; we are weak—you are strong. We are only simple Indians—you have knowledge and wisdom in your head; we need your help and your protection. We no longer have a homeland—no livestock—no land, and we will soon no longer need anything. Soon the wind will blow over the last homes our fathers owned. I am very concerned about this, but I cannot turn away our fate. The sun, the moon, the rivers, the forests, which are so dear to me, these we must leave. Soon we will sleep under the ground—and awake no more. My father, I have nothing more to say to you."

Our narrator fell into deep silence. In Owaissa's lovely eyes gleamed a tear, and the dark fate of her red brothers stood before her troubled soul more painful than ever.

****

With these words, the text breaks off, leaving a highly emotional impression on the reader. Anneke brings immediacy to her reports and descriptions by writing in the first person and carrying the reader along into the scene she describes with intriguing detail. Using the format of a travelogue, she also reveals a very personal point of view, often using a familiar, conversational tone. The reader sees a positive, poetic description of Milwaukee and Lake Michigan, indicating perhaps her own positive feelings about the United States, at least when viewed from overseas. Anneke often found herself torn between homesickness for Europe and especially for Germany where she was born, and attachment to her new life in the United States. She decided to join her husband in Switzerland at the time of the Civil War in part because of that homesickness, and in part to have the family together again. However, her feelings for her new home in Wisconsin remained, and she did, of course, decide to return there for the last part of her life.

In the nineteenth century, women writers often used travelogues with a dual purpose. Traveling outside of their homeland gave women a new context for considerations of social issues. By bringing in customs and attitudes from another culture, the woman writer could more easily examine the assumptions of her own culture. Louise Büchner, for example, wrote a travelogue in 1875, "Eine Reise-Erinnerung" ("A Travel Memoir"), reflecting on her trip to Switzerland. Some of the text reveals personal thoughts and emotions evoked by the memories of her brother. However, in the context of this trip and family memories, Büchner interjects a consideration of the Swiss university system, which was admitting women to study medicine on an equal basis with men. This description of the university system, and its implied contrast with the German university system that resisted admitting women, also allowed Büchner to write about the whole social question of balancing a professional career and raising a family.

Anneke's travelogue functions in much the same way. She is ostensibly describing Lake Michigan and Milwaukee, and indeed she does include visual descriptions, which are often very poetic. The beauty of the natural environment is a perfect backdrop for her consideration of social issues dear to her heart. The beginning of her article immediately makes reference to her antislavery sentiment and her feelings of support for a man who would take forceful action to protect a slave. In addition, the majestic view of the city and the shore along with the open lake contrasts with the prison fortress, the marble Bastille, as she calls it. It is impossible to miss the irony she feels in the contrast of the United States as a symbol of freedom while being a legal enforcer of the rights of slaveholders. She emphasizes her point visually for her readers by describing the noble Stars and Stripes flying alongside of the white cloth waved by her imprisoned friend from the small window of his cell.

With Anneke's antislavery attitude prominently placed at the beginning of her article, she then introduces exotic information about the founding of the city of Milwaukee and about the indigenous people. Part two introduces the Winnebaga chieftain who is portrayed with a disarming simplicity in his desire to own one of the chandelier crystals. For the modern reader, the picture of this man is only partly positive. He seems like a child, and the reader might well fear for his fate at the hands of the white settlers of the area. The contrast with Owaissa, who is part Indian and part European, is interesting. She is the same type of "synthesis" introduced in "Uhland in Texas" in the character Indianna. The noblest of Anneke's "noble savages" seems to be the individual living in both cultures. Indeed, she further makes that clear through her introduction of the young man reared by a Native American foster mother. By blood he is European, but culturally he also lives in both worlds.

In part three, Anneke's compassion for the plight of the native tribes comes through as she presents a scene where a proud Chippewa chieftain presents directly his tribe's miserable situation in resigned, unadorned language. It is characteristic of Anneke that she uses her prose to move her audience emotionally as well as intellectually when she presents a social situation of suffering and oppression. And indeed, the article makes its greatest impact on the emotional level through the depiction of a silent tear in the eyes of the noble Owaissa.

Notes

1. The text in German appeared in the indicated newspaper in January 1864. I have translated representative excerpts in this chapter. The complete text (in German) is available in: Anneke, Mathilde Franziska. *Die gebrochenen Ketten: Erzählungen, Reportagen und Reden (1861–1873)*. Maria Wagner, ed. (and postscript). Stuttgart: Hans-Dieter Heinz Akademischer Verlag, 1983.

2. Anneke writes *Marmorbastille* alluding to the famous Bastille in Paris as a symbol of the struggle for freedom and the ideals of the French Revolution. She uses every opportunity to contrast the supposed freedom in the United States and the existence of slavery.

3. Anneke uses an asterisk and notes: Chicago and Cincinnati contend with her [Milwaukee] for the crown of "Queen of the West."

4. Anneke writes these quoted words in English, adding to the "American-ness" of the piece for her readers. The same is true of her use of Native American terms and her interest in the derivations of place names in the indigenous languages.

5. I use this translation to reflect Anneke's nineteenth-century use of *Rothäute* (literally "redskins")—or, indeed, she may have been trying to reflect the old captain's terminology. In other parts of the text, she refers to red men and Indians interchangeably.

6. The vocabulary referring to the Native Americans appears in Anneke's original text.

7. The *Adelsbrief* referred to in the text is a letter testifying as to an individual's family background.

8. Anneke's footnote translates: the name in the Indian language for "white American."

Chapter 6

In Her Own Words: Mathilde Franziska Anneke's Defense of Women's Rights

Defending her political point of view by the force of her pen and in public speeches was always part of Mathilde Franziska Anneke's activist life. Even her appreciation of literature was connected with its contribution to political causes and the individual liberty she valued so much. Maria Wagner notes, for example, that two outlines for discussions of German literature, prepared for speeches to be delivered in Milwaukee in 1850, clearly revealed Anneke's interest in *"engagierte Literatur"* (*Feminismus, Literatur und Revolution* 121, 128). Included in Henrietta M. Heinzen's biographical notes in the Anneke Papers in the Wisconsin Historical Society, there is another example, a reference to a lecture from April 16, 1850, entitled "Political Events and Poetry in Germany" (33), establishing once again Mathilde Anneke's activist view of literature. Her early revolutionary writing also showed her great talent as a journalist, and even when she wrote fiction, her stories gave expression to social wrongs. Her major focus was women's rights and the antislavery question. In "Die Gebrochenen Ketten" ("Broken Chains"), discussed and translated in Chapter 7, Anneke combines both issues as she presents the horror of slavery from a young woman's point of view. Her central character, Lelia, is subject to the young master's sexual predation because of her dual disadvantage as woman and slave.

Mathilde Franziska Anneke's contributions to the Woman Suffrage Movement in its early years have been noted in volume I (1848–1861) of *The History of Woman Suffrage*, edited by Elizabeth Cady Stanton, Susan B.

Anthony, and Matilda Joslyn Gage. Although Anneke was still in Germany when the Woman Suffrage Movement had its start at the Seneca Falls Convention of 1848, she and her husband were soon forced to flee into exile because of their revolutionary activities and the defeat of liberal forces on the battlefield. Heinzen's biographical notes detail the beginning of Anneke's work in America for women's rights by including a translation of parts of a letter to Alexander Jonas.[1] Anneke writes:

> ...After my flight to this country with my husband, the strivings of many American women became known to me; I read the excellent articles of Elizabeth Oakes Smith[2], translated her works as well as the fiery arguments of Elizabeth Cady Stanton and Susan B. Anthony against certain parts of the Common Law before the Legislature in Albany for German journals, which were formerly friendly to me, but found no reception anywhere. I learned to prize highly the efforts of Fanny Wright, Lucretia Mott, Ernestine L. Rose, Pauline Davis[3] and others and to strengthen myself by means of them. I wrote the first number of my Frauenztg [*Frauenzeitung*] here in distant west alone and untroubled about any possible consequences. It appeared on March 1, 1852... (34)

Anneke goes on to write about her attempt to form an organization of German women, and offered her newspaper as the tool for communicating ideas. Then she writes about speaking in various cities to large audiences. She mentions Chicago, Cleveland, Buffalo, and New York. From Boston, she was invited to give further lectures. Her trip was a long and challenging one. Several paragraphs later in the same letter, she writes:

> After a dangerous trip of several days and nights through the Alleghenies I reached Cincinnati where Gottfried Kinkel had just stirred the German element. Here in Turnhall an exceedingly large audience received me, and I won lively applause for my always decidedly outspoken demands. I gave several lectures here and then turned to Louisville, where I continued my agitation as guest of several known and unknown friends, and received from women especially signs of encouragement and agreement such as had not yet been bestowed on me up to this time. They had heard that it was my wish to own a small printing office. The gold pieces intended for a medal were not cast but were handed to me 'in nature' for that purpose. My trip extended up by way of Dayton, Pittsburgh, etc. (35)

On this tour, Anneke's lectures were directed at a German-speaking audience. It was only in 1853 when she spoke to the Women's Rights Convention in New York that she entered into the mainstream Woman Suffrage Movement. Her lectures to this immigrant audience were provocative, challenging the strictures forced on women by government and religion. Two examples show the focus of her content. In Philadelphia (October 2, 1852), she gave a speech with the title "Freie und sittliche Erhebung des weiblichen Geschlechts" ("Free and Ethical Rebellion of the Female Sex"), and on October 25 she spoke on the "Verbesserung der Lage der Frau" ("Improvement of the Condition of Woman") (Wagner, *MFA in Selbstzeugnissen* 324–325).

Anneke's newspaper is mentioned in volume 1 of *The History of Woman Suffrage*, Chapter 2: Women in Newspapers. Her first newspaper experience occurred while she was still in Germany, but once in the United States she continued to wish to lend her journalistic talent to support the battle for women's rights. Her *Deutsche Frauen-Zeitung*, which appeared in March 1852 in Milwaukee, was the first feminist paper published by a woman in the United States (Wagner, *MFA in Selbstzeugnissen* 315). In the letter to Alexander Jonas referred to above, Anneke mentions moving back east from Wisconsin in December and purchasing a printing office. She notes: "I hoped gradually to set the type with women's hands, a plan which had failed in Wisconsin" (Heinzen 35). Her next paragraph discusses the type of articles contained in her paper:

> Henceforth my paper appeared weekly and indeed from Newark, after several wanderings in New York and Jersey City. Up to that time I had published stimulating material in it, excerpts from Hippel[4], translations from Mary Wollstonecraft, Margaret Fuller and others. I had given my own opinions in my lectures, and reprinted 'Das Weib im Konflikt mit den Sozialen Verhaeltnissen.'[5] (Fragments of it were also later printed in the Kriminalztg. now the Belletristische). I kept faithful watch on the events of the movement which had been called into being by the American champions, and reported on the social ambitions of the then workers' clubs in New York, Williamsburg, and Newark, where I also gave lectures. I there advocated my view that the social question could only be solved by the emancipation of woman. (Heinzen 35)

Mathilde Franziska Anneke's skill in writing demonstrates her persuasive abilities in defense of women (see Chapter 3 for the complete text of "Das Weib im Conflict mit den Socialen Verhältnissen," translated as "Woman in Conflict with Society") and in support of the Anti-Slavery Movement (see Chapter 7). However, perhaps her greatest skill was in public speaking. She was able to stand before audiences, especially German immigrant audiences, and evoke some of the same passion she herself felt for human rights. It is hard to capture that skill without resorting to modern devices such as recordings or video. However, she did leave draft copies of two speeches from the period after her return to the United States from Switzerland in 1865, which Maria Wagner included in her book, *Die gebrochenen Ketten: Erzählungen, Reportagen und Reden (1861–1873)*. These supply the modern reader with readable, German-language copies of material otherwise not easily accessible. Both drafts are excellent examples of what must have been inspiring speeches when delivered before an audience.

The first speech from 1872 was for the opening of the German Hall in Milwaukee and concerns equal rights for women (Wagner 219–222; the translation is mine):

***

On the Occasion of the Inauguration of the German Hall in Milwaukee (Concerning Equal Rights for Women)

Since the earliest times of humanity, the female sex has found herself in a position of servitude in relation to men. What greater manly vigor and strength could boast of—which was merely a physical fact,—soon became a legal right, and it was given the sanction of society, which fundamentally attempted to make this inequality, this obedience legal. Woman entered into bondage. This slavery became law, and the male side came to an agreement to protect each other mutually in the possession of their gain. In earlier times most males were also slaves like all females. Centuries passed before a philosopher stepped forward to question the right and absolute necessity of slavery. Little by little, chosen intellects and people of strong character arose, who supported the general progress of society, lifted the slavery of men completely, and changed the slavery of women into a milder form of dependence. This dependence, although milder and less harsh, as the customs and relations of human beings with each other have become generally more fair and humane, is still an intrinsic and undeniable condition of subjugation. Whoever has the right taken away to live life according to one's own law, that person lives under the control of another, dependent on his determination and will—that person is not free!

Unjust institutions lead to the debasement of human hearts. No one knows human nature without knowing that whoever possesses power—and let him be the most noble-minded person—watches over this power to the nth degree with Argus eyes, and enjoys the feel of his possession, the use of this power often far too much.

Among those who are by nature crude and the least educated morally, the legal subordination of women, along with the fact that they are physically subjugated to his will, brings forth a feeling of contempt on the part of the husband toward his own wife. And we find this situation not only among men without good breeding and education. Indeed just recently a whole group of men—men who ought to represent the good breeding of the German homeland, furnished proof of their lack of inherent respect for women, even for mothers. I won't even mention the vile behavior of the press in our country. Surely even in our German papers we can daily come across enough examples where the noblest, most unselfish efforts of women earn payment in scorn, ridicule, and statements of all kinds. It is characteristic that you will find in such journals the most eloquent language for the most obvious necessity of a particular reform for women's suffering and lot, and right away in another column you will find preparation of such a reform disdained and slandered with the favorite quotation marks in the text. Is that humanity and justice which we are appealing to, you representatives of freedom? Unjust institutions lead by their nature to debasement of the human heart, and we recognize clearly that we will never and in no way, no matter how mildly the scepter of power by the mercy of God and men is wielded, befriend institutions which are diametrically opposed to the principle of sacred freedom—which are opposed to human rights and human dignity.... To you, representatives of freedom, who will only find your own full enjoyment of that freedom when you no longer tolerate any inequality about you, to you do I want to appeal with the full conviction and enthusiasm of my heart. Set woman free. Raise her to a true educator of humanity, to the defender of your freedom... If you widen the sphere of her activity, you double the intelligence in service of humanity. And what with full right belongs to you, do not let half of it go unused. You have no excess of skills and talents. Give woman the consciousness of being a free person equal to other free people who have the right to choose for themselves their purpose in life. Do not feed us with references to your chivalry, your protection! Do not point us to the sphere of the household, the private hearth. Millions and millions of my sex have no home, no hearth. Millions, I tell you! Look over toward Albion's dynastic wavering shore, there the population count just finished shows a million more of my people than of yours. Yes, New England counts in the thousands. In Germany and France the ratio does not seem more advantageous, where Krupp's cannons and machine guns have produced *tabula rasa* with the male flower of humanity, and where the women wither after them in double numbers.

Join the best minds of your time and fight for equal rights—the last, the most holy fight. May you not be reproached because you, Germans whose forefathers adored love and freedom equally in Freya, goddess of the Sacred Grove, could court someone other than a free maiden.

And now to you womanly hearts, prepare yourselves for the day of redemption. It's coming! The barrier between our life of subjugation and the life of reasonable freedom is falling. The day of humanity's cultural and intellectual betterment begins in truth with *our* freedom, if our relationships in life stand under the law of equal justice, and we learn as people to cultivate our strongest feelings with people who stand equal to us in rights and duties. It begins when we gain self worth and become as highly valued as we should be... Injustice, which determines the matter, ceases: we could, from birth and by virtue of the same, be incapable of those occupations which are open to the lowest of the other sex, or we might—no matter how capable we are, stay away from their practice so that the exclusive advantage would be granted to men. People will no longer praise the lesser intellectual capability of our sex—no one seriously believes that any more anyway—because in the struggles of public life—from which women are not excluded, our talent has been tested. We have passed the test! We no longer believe the soothing words, which seek to make us understand that everything is happening for our benefit, without us determining what our benefit is. Looking around us, we are aware of no superabundance of people who are qualified to complete educated work so that society could afford to refuse our service. We will be allowed to compete for the practice of our duties, and we will not force ourselves into professions in which we are subordinate to [other] competitors. We will also prefer professions in which we have no competition. We will be mothers, wives, and teachers [raisers of children], and will only truly and rightly fulfill our profession as wife and mother when we have the freedom to choose our profession and be responsible for it. We will have to be trusted with functions of an official nature; we will have to be allowed, as women citizens among [all the] citizens of these free states, to take part in the election of those persons to whom public office shall be entrusted. Possession of a voice in the general election is a means of self-protection, which must belong to each person by right, a guarantee of a person's welfare, a guarantee of intellectual and cultural elevation, a symbol of equal rights, the fortune of our time.

In four years our adopted fatherland, whose daughters and proudly aware citizens we are, will celebrate, our republic will celebrate her one-hundredth birthday. Prepare yourselves for this celebration of freedom. It will be a day of atonement, a day of the greatest glory. The signs of the time do not deceive us.

Prepare your halls, beautiful like this one, which you have just built. Decorate them with oak leaves and myrtle for the bridal day of full independence. Build in places like this one, the palladium of the people, full of light and beautiful, and lower your voice in the inviolate vessel. Because bathed in the magic of harmonies, whose agents we wish to become, we strive together with you, you dear men, agents of freedom, toward the happiness of [all] humanity.

***

This draft for her speech shows her focus on the vote for women and her confidence that it would soon been obtained. She, unfortunately, would not live to see the passage of the Nineteenth Amendment. She did spend many years speaking and writing in support of the suffrage issue. Her hopes for some sort of declaration during the July 4, 1876, celebration were not totally disappointed. She and several other suffrage leaders prepared a Declaration of Rights, which carries Mathilde Franziska Anneke's signature along with thirty others including well-known suffragists Lucretia Mott, Elizabeth Cady Stanton, Ernestine L. Rose, Susan B. Anthony, Matilda Joslyn Gage, and Olympia Brown.[6] The opening paragraph is full of hope and grievance:

> While the nation is buoyant with patriotism, and all hearts are attuned to praise, it is with sorrow we come to strike the one discordant note, on this one-hundredth anniversary of our country's birth. When subjects of kings, emperors, and czars, from the old world join in our national jubilee, shall the women of the republic refuse to lay their hands with benedictions on the nation's head? Surveying America's exposition, surpassing in magnificence those of London, Paris, and Vienna, shall we not rejoice at the success of the youngest rival among the nations of the earth? May not our hearts, in unison with all, swell with pride at our great achievement as a people; our free speech, free press, free schools, free church, and the rapid progress we have made in material wealth, trade, commerce and the inventive arts? And we do rejoice in the success, thus far, of our experiment of self-government. Our faith is firm and unwavering in the broad principles of human rights proclaimed in 1776, not only as abstract truths, but as the corner stones of a republic. Yet we cannot forget, even in this glad hour, that while all men of every race, and clime, and condition, have been invested with the full rights of citizenship under our hospitable flag, all women still suffer the degradation of disfranchisement. (Frost & Cullen-DuPont 396–397)

The document then traces a "series of assumptions and usurpations of power over woman, in direct opposition to the principles of just government," using the format of a series of articles of impeachment (397–398), and arguing that "national safety and stability" depend on redressing this wrong against one-half of the nation's people. The closing declaration is that woman was made for her own happiness, not to be sacrificed to man's happiness, and not to have her interests sacrificed to his will. But they also stress that they are only asking for what is their due as American citizens. With these dramatic words, they close their Declaration: "We ask of our rulers, at this hour, no special favors, no special privileges, no special legislation. We ask justice, we ask equality, we ask that all the civil and political rights that belong to citizens of the United States be guaranteed to us and our daughters forever" (399).

Anneke distinguished herself in her strong and immediate support of the suffragists shortly after her arrival in the United States. She attended many of the conventions, including the famous Mob Convention in New York, and corresponded with suffrage leaders including Susan B. Anthony.[7] When the Woman Suffrage Movement split into the National Woman Suffrage Association (NWSA) and the American Woman Suffrage Association (AWSA)— over the Fifteenth Amendment as well as other issues, such as the inclusion of men in the movement, and whether suffrage alone, or a whole range of women's issues should be addressed (Frost & Cullen-DuPont 177)—Anneke remained loyal to Anthony and Stanton and the NWSA. She defended Elizabeth Cady Stanton in writing in the German press when she was accused of anti-immigrant sentiments, and gave a speech in defense of Susan B. Anthony on July 13, 1873, following Anthony's arrest for voting. Both compositions show the power of Anneke's written and spoken word. Indeed, her written essays often have the feel of an impassioned speech.

The draft for Anneke's speech of 1873 follows (Wagner *Die gebrochenen Ketten* 223–226; the translation is mine):

The Conviction of Susan B. Anthony

There is no greater hindrance, which still stands in the way of the betterment of conditions in general, no worse obstacle, upon which the improvement and higher perfection of humanity runs aground, no more brutal injustice, which weighs on the great conscience of today's society—than the legal subordination of one sex to the other.

The most highly praised position of woman is, according to the concepts of human dignity and general human rights, not a fitting one; the seemingly most secure position is only a precarious one, constantly hovering in danger; the seemingly most cultured position subject to all types of arbitrariness, as long as it can be ruled by the will and discretion of others. Equal rights before the law gives her an ethical stability; her participation in legislation a firm, legal base; the use of the vote the guarantee of permanence.

Equal rights are bound to raise the female sex out of her feeling of degradation and dependence to consciousness of equality and self-determination; they will raise her to her human dignity. This participation in legislation must make woman responsible for the regulation of political and social questions of our times and empowers her to eliminate injustices, and to abolish the unfairness that prevails everywhere in the laws against her. The right to vote will give her the power to be included in all public matters and to have a deciding voice in questions which are her own most immediate interests, such as marriage and marriage laws, education and children's rights. Her right to vote must be a protection for reborn integrity in the life of the state, and a defense against every type of corruption. It shall awaken enthusiasm and interest in the most precious possessions in human life, and through the activity which is connected to public interest, shall free woman from the frivolous and childish trifles, the idleness and false directions in life which have held her captive up until now. It must also free her from the bonds by which she was still controlled to some extent by the priesthood and church, and to which dark powers she was consigned in stubborn egoism by the mighty of the earth in spite of progressive scientific enlightenment. It should lead her from blind faith and prejudice to thoughtful activity, which will give her practical stability and vitality and that triumphant conviction of being able to achieve, through her own energy, her own education, and her own sound judgment, a life worthy of a human being, which is no longer consoled by heaven and the afterlife.

For equal rights and its demonstration through general suffrage, for this palladium of a free people, the women of this country have struggled for longer than a quarter century. Unshakeable through continual challenges, through the most zealous publicity, and through the most skillful argumentation that exhausted all doubt, they have forced respect and a closer examination of the question from their opponents. They have personally proven before Congress that the principles, upon which the proud structure of the Union rests, are lies and its institutions are idle boasting, as long as they exclude the greater half of its citizens from participation in legislation and hold them in subordination to the other half. They have induced judicious statesmen to examine their claims, and prevailed upon Congress as well as [state] legislatures to make the attempt to amend their respective constitutions, and possibly modify them along these lines: to strike the word "male," which refers to privileged citizens, completely from their texts. Finally, they have persuaded the greatest philosophers and men of science from all countries to honor the truth and to publicize the irrefutable knowledge that woman is also part of humanity.

After all these results, which the oppressed themselves—understand rightly, the downtrodden themselves—have wrested from those in power, after a quarter century of tireless work and effort on the part of women, it seemed about time, on the basis of the interpretation of various amendments in favor of equal rights, especially of women with men—indeed it seemed imperative to ask the opinion of the judiciary, that holy oracle which should be the voice, not of God, but of the people, the voice of their clear conception of justice—whether at long last mercy might come forth, and woman might be allowed self-determination in regard to her own welfare and participation in legislation. This question was made into a test case. Through such so-called test cases, it has always occurred with regard to questions of principle in the United States that they are brought to a conclusive interpretation, to an arbitration in which the representatives of the principles consent to give a factual explanation, and let the distinguished judges decide, to judge not according to the rigid letter of the law, but according to the concept of justice supported and purified by the spirit of the time.

Susan B. Anthony, that bright, courageous, unselfish, ever-ready fighter for radical principles of every type, threw herself into the breach. She did it because of the most deeply felt impulse of her serious, tireless aspiration, of her most sacred conviction. She did it to test the reality of the words, which were nothing but hypocritical words, of that corrupt party which called itself the ruling party, and which knew how to make itself into the victorious party through the help of women.

She cast her vote in good faith. She voted conscious of an imperative duty as a citizen of the United States, as representative of a great human principle. She placed her ballot in the urn with permission of the inspectors on duty at the site, who were persuaded of the right of women to vote. She cast it, encouraged by the opinion of a sitting legislator, whom she asked and who had stated that the right is irrefutable. She had reason to hope, if she were hauled into court to answer for her glorious deed, that the truth of her principle, for which she and the best women of our country have fought, which has been sanctioned by the middle and upper classes of our people and of other people, might also prevail in the hearts of the judges, and might be raised to a test case through their noble degree. She was mistaken. The middle and upper classes were mistaken with her. She was convicted because she voted and—is only a woman!

If she had stolen up to the voting urn, if she had voted ten times at once, if she had voted falsely—if only she had not come as a woman!—she would not have been convicted. But no, no, no, she voted correctly; she voted honestly, she voted with the noblest intentions that have ever impelled a heart to vote—she, a woman, voted, and was thrown into prison, was convicted. It is too late, says the *Cincinnati Commercial*, to speak of limiting or abridging the right to vote by census, level of education, or race. All of these barriers have been broken down. We have tried the experiment of universal suffrage, so far as men are concerned. The arena is widening with the progress of civilization, until everyone is included, without discrimination based on race, ability, or other conditions. Only women, the mentally disabled, and criminals are excluded! Day after day, year after year, women have shown their abilities for public official duties and proven their right [to them]. There is almost no profession any longer in which we have not seen women as successful representatives. The arts and sciences count among their most illustrious younger members excellent women. They have talents in the practical activities of life, [and] in carrying out great enterprises. They are competent accountants, faithful assistants, and intelligent financiers. The fact that there are many among them who own property and administer it intelligently proves their good sense. Why should they not be permitted to cast their ballot in an election? What reasons does the state have to deny equal participation to its citizens?

***

In the archives of the Anneke Collection in the Wisconsin Historical Society, there is an undated newspaper clipping (December 31, 18—) with a reprint of Mathilde Anneke's defense of Elizabeth Cady Stanton. A reader had written in to the newspaper (the *Nordstern*) that Mrs. Stanton had said in a speech that women in Germany are hitched to a yoke with cattle or oxen to work the fields. This accusation provided an opportunity for a very interesting response by Anneke, directed at the German immigrant community. Although she responds to the immediate accusation, she also touches on the question of American nativism. The text in translation reads as follows:

On the Women's Rights Movement

[There is an introductory paragraph explaining that this open letter to the *Nordstern* by Mathilde Anneke comes in response to a letter by a Mr. Tillmann related to a speech given by Mrs. Elizabeth Cady Stanton in La Crosse, Wisconsin. The reprint omits a few of her introductory words and then offers the remainder of the text.]

You were so kind, Mr. Tillmann, as to inform me in your letter that Mrs. Elizabeth Cady Stanton held a lecture on "Woman Rights" on the evening of the 26th before a large audience in La Crosse, and there not only set forth a nativistic prejudice with the use of the words "ignorant foreigners," but even worse uttered the following words, which I give in German translation:

"Isn't it really absurd that the right to vote is granted, in this land to which he immigrates, to the ignorant German, who in his homeland yokes his wife to the plow next to his oxen or his cow, and as a result he is allowed to make laws for the educated and intelligent women of America?"

You further inform me in your letter that, upon closer questioning as to the verification of the first part of her phrase, Mrs. Stanton was relying not on various travelogues, but rather on me and my information about the fact, and you request, on behalf of several Germans from La Crosse, that I provide information about the above-mentioned situation.

That claim by Mrs. Stanton is a rhetorical metaphor, which was used to show graphically that the immigrant of lower cultural standing, who neither knows the free institutions of this country, nor appreciates them, indeed that man, who in his homeland is legally allowed to keep his wife in slavery* [Anneke adds a footnote at the end of the page that reads: "Prussian law grants the husband the right to punish his wedded wife, to beat her as long as he does not thereby endanger her life, i.e., as long as he does not strike her dead."], comes here and, as a naturalized, sovereign citizen, rules over every American woman without the right to vote. That is, due to his right to vote, he becomes her lawgiver.

Whether I have ever conceded the bare truth of the premises of that statement, as she said, I don't know, and it really doesn't matter because whenever and wherever there has been an opportunity, I have stated bluntly that woman, not only in Germany but in all countries and at all times, has experienced a much deeper degradation and privation due to the lack in her legal standing, than she could suffer through burdens imposed, even by the lowest and most difficult work. I have never considered dishonorable the honest, justly shared work of a wife with her husband, whether in front of or behind the plow, whether next to an ox or a cow—even if it is dishonorable for the arrangement of human society because of its difficulty or form,— never have I considered the person dishonorable. Under some conditions, in Germany, the land of social grievances, such a division of labor appeared quite often of imperative necessity to spare oneself and the family from ruin and want. Not without some feelings of sadness, I still remember today based on my own observation and experience the most hopeless scenes from my beloved fatherland, and not without horror [I still remember today] what an extremely heavy portion of that burden weighs down my poor sex. These conditions, not any less heart-breaking, which come from poverty and suffering, are as hopeless as those due to the legal subordination of one sex to the other, an injustice in and of itself, and an inhibition of higher perfection, indeed a dishonor to human dignity. Compared with the dark phantoms of vice and unhappiness, of tears and suffering, which hide everywhere behind purple curtains as well as in cottages and dens of misery in European cities, and which take place with the sanction of legal institutions—Elizabeth Cady Stanton's image must look like a touching, indeed "rustic customs" idyll of our German homeland.

Why Elizabeth Cady Stanton illustrates the absurdity of the anti-republican institutions in this country with "ignorant foreigners" and not with the crude and ignorant men of her own country, I do not know. In any case, she seemed to intend to set very boldly in the eyes of her countrymen the injustice of inequality before the law, using the most glaring contradiction. Moreover, she has only a certain class of immigrants in view—namely the uneducated, since she specifically refers to "ignorant foreigners," not "foreigners." The educated group of Germans has, as I'm sure you will understand, no reason at all to complain about her; on the contrary, she turns to them with special trust in their strong support of the urgent question of the time, "political equality without distinction based on race, color and sex," which, just like in its time the Reformation, or the abolition of burning people alive and serfdom, or like the emancipation of the Jews and slaves, is a historical necessity, and which must and will very soon come to pass under the sun of this enlightened century.

This truth should be obvious to the German-American citizen, who is raised and nurtured on the spirit of German philosophy, and he should not, in petty irritation unworthy of him, take a position against the lofty idea of the principle of complete equality and its serious scientific testing.

Please accept, honorable sir, my high esteem and my thanks for the opportunity you have given me, with the full warmth of my conviction and with the love, which I maintain continually in exile for my beloved fatherland, to direct a word of admonition to my beloved countrymen. Do not close your eyes and ears to the sign of the times, rather look forward with open and joyous eyes to the newly arriving period in this world as it is worthy of the daughters and sons of our beautiful Germany, and of the philosophical spirit of its poets and thinkers, which nowhere surrounds us so clearly and foretelling as in this country, in which at least the seed for freedom has been sown, and which the sun of equality permits to grow into a tree, in whose shade humanity shall become beautiful and happy.

Mathilde Franziska Anneke

However, perhaps her most dramatic moment came early in her association with the suffrage movement at the famous Mob Convention in New York at the Broadway Tabernacle (September 6 & 7, 1853), reported in *The History of Woman Suffrage*, volume 1 (571–573). During this Woman's Rights Convention, Paulina Wright Davis offered a resolution: "*Resolved*, That inasmuch as this great movement is intended to meet the wants, not of America only, but of the whole world, a committee be appointed to prepare an address from this Convention to the women of Great Britain and the continent of Europe, setting forth our objects, and inviting their co-operation in the same" (570). The committee included Mathilde Franziska Anneke. She also spoke at this unusual convention, which was repeatedly interrupted by a mob of opposing voices who planned to interrupt the proceedings by making it impossible for speakers to be heard. *The History of Woman Suffrage* reports Anneke's brief remarks, introducing them this way:

> The President then introduced a German lady, Madame Mathilde Franziska Anneke, editor of a liberal woman's rights newspaper which had been suppressed in Germany. She had but recently landed in our country, and hastened to the Convention to

enjoy the blessings of free speech in a republic. She had heard so much of freedom in America, that she could hardly express her astonishment at what she witnessed. After many attempts, and with great difficulty, owing to the tumult and interruption by impertinent noises, she spoke as follows, in German, Mrs. [Ernestine L.] Rose translating her remarks into English:

"I wish to say only a few words. On the other side of the Atlantic there is no freedom of any kind, and we have not even the right to claim freedom of speech. But can it be that here, too, there are tyrants who violate the individual right to express opinions on any subject? And do you call yourselves republicans? No; there is no republic without freedom of speech." [There is continued interruption. Wendell Phillips speaks of Anneke's revolutionary activities in Europe and attempts to calm the crowd by appealing to their self-respect as citizens of America.]

"I saw this morning, in a paper, that the women of America have met in convention to claim their rights. I rejoiced when I saw that they recognized their equality; and I rejoiced when I saw that they have not forgotten their sisters in Germany. I wished to be here with my American sisters, to tell them that I sympathize in their efforts; but I was too sick to come, and would probably not have been here but that another German woman, a friend of this movement, came to Newark and took me out of my sick bed. But it was the want of a knowledge of the English language which kept me away, more than sickness.

"Before I came here, I knew the tyranny and oppression of kings; I felt it in my own person, and friends, and country; and when I came here I expected to find that freedom which is denied us at home. Our sisters in Germany have long desired freedom, but there the desire is repressed as well in man as in woman. There is no freedom there, even to claim human rights. Here they expect to find freedom of speech; here, for if we can not claim it here, where should we go for it? Here, at least, we ought to be able to express our opinions on all subjects; and yet, it would appear, there is no freedom even here to claim human rights, although the only hope in our country for freedom of speech and action, is directed to this country for illustration and example. That freedom I claim. The women of my country look to this for encouragement and sympathy; and they, also, sympathize with this cause. We hope it will go on and prosper; and many hearts across the ocean in Germany are beating in unison with those here."

This speech marked Anneke's entry into the mainstream suffrage movement where, except for a brief period when she was in Switzerland during the Civil War, she remained active until her death. Indeed, Mathilde Anneke became a symbol of the connection between women's rights movements in Europe and the movement in the United States. Her faith in the leaders of the National Woman Suffrage Association was unwavering, and her rhetoric and arguments for women's rights in the broadest sense, and especially for the right to vote, remained fiery and radical throughout her life. Unlike some of the Forty-Eighters, her political activism and liberal ideas did not moderate with time, and she always believed in the rightness of the women's movement. From the texts presented in this chapter, Anneke aptly demonstrates both her views and her loyalty to Susan B. Anthony and Elizabeth Cady Stanton. Her admiration for their efforts was reciprocated, and the Anneke Collection in Madison, Wisconsin, contains some of the letters of their correspondence. A letter from Susan B. Anthony from September 27, 1875, addressed to "My Dear Friend Madam Anneke" discusses NWSA matters (the idea of a "grand mass meeting of indignation and protest" in Philadelphia on July 4, 1876, for example[8]) in the confiding style of a friend and equal in the struggle. One paragraph illustrates directly Anthony's regard when she writes: "I am glad you do not get discouraged with the seeming neglect of Mrs. Stanton or me—but it's seeming—for I am interested in all you say—always—& shall ever be grateful for all your thought for me personally in my efforts to establish the principle of woman's equality of rights."

Anneke's ideals of freedom and equality flourished on American soil, and her passion for the cause of woman suffrage and women's rights can be seen in her later writings and speeches as well as her early ones. Finally, in 1865, her belief in reform and the power of education brought her to the last major project of her life, the founding of a school for young women in Milwaukee.

NOTES

1. I have retained Heinzen's punctuation throughout these quotes from her typescript.
2. Elizabeth Oakes Smith (1806–1893). American author and prominent advocate of women's rights. Her book *Woman and Her Needs* was published in 1851.
3. Fanny Wright (Frances Wright) (1795–1852), U.S. abolitionist and social reformer for women's rights, born in Scotland; known as a freethinker, writer, and public speaker. Lucretia Mott (1793–1880), well-known U.S. social reformer and advocate of women's rights. Ernestine L. Rose (1810–1892), Polish-born reformer, and early advocate for women's rights and for the abolition of slavery in the United States. Pauline Davis (Paulina Wright Davis) (1813–1876), American reformer and suffragist; in the late 1830s she joined E. Rose in petitioning the New York legislature for a married women's property law.
4. Theodor Gottlieb von Hippel published his pivotal work, *Über die bürgerliche Verbesserung der Weiber* (*On the Civil Improvement of Women*) in 1792. In this work he argued that women should have opportunities equal to those of men in education and employment outside of the domestic sphere, enabling them to become full members of society.

5. This more modern spelling of the essay's title was used in Heinzen's typed manuscript.

6. The full list reads: Lucretia Mott, Elizabeth Cady Stanton, Paulina Wright Davis, Ernestine L. Rose, Clarina I.H. Nichols, Mary Ann McClintock, Mathilde Franceske Anneke, Sarah Pugh, Amy Post, Catharine A.F. Stebbins, Susan B. Anthony, Matilda Joslyn Gage, Clemence S. Lozier, Olympia Brown, Mathilde F. Wendt, Adeline Thomson, Ellen Clark Sargent, Virginia L. Minor, Catherine V. Waite, Elizabeth B. Schenck, Phoebe W. Couzins, Elizabeth Boynton Harbert, Laura De-Force Gordon, Sara Andrews Spencer, Lillie Devereux Blake, Jane Graham Jones, Abigail Scott Duniway, Belva A. Lockwood, Isabella Beecher Hooker, Sarah L. Williams, and Abby P. Ela.

7. Letters from Susan B. Anthony to Mathilde Anneke are preserved in the Anneke Collection at the Wisconsin Historical Society in Madison, Wisconsin. Some also appear in Maria Wagner, *Mathilde Franziska Anneke in Selbstzeugnissen und Dokumenten* in German translation.

8. This "meeting of indignation" is discussed at the beginning of a postscript to the letter of Sept. 27, 1875.

Chapter 7

The Anti-Slavery Movement and Anneke's "Broken Chains"

For many nineteenth-century women activists, participation in the Woman Suffrage Movement came about as a result of earlier contact, and often involvement, with the Anti-Slavery Movement. This was certainly true of Lucretia Mott and Elizabeth Cady Stanton, who attended the World Anti-Slavery Convention in London during the summer of 1840 as part of the U.S. delegation, and found themselves relegated to the galleries as observers while only the male delegates were seated.[1] Susan B. Anthony was also a strong advocate of the abolition of slavery, as were many others who later fought for women's rights. Through contact with suffrage leaders, especially Stanton and Anthony, upon her arrival in the United States, Mathilde Franziska Anneke quickly became aware of the issues and rhetoric involved. The ideals and sympathies developed during her participation in the Revolution of 1848 in Germany and her sensitivity to social injustices would not allow her to accept or ignore the practice of slavery. In fact, work in the Anti-Slavery Movement was often the catalyst, confirming in women's (and some men's) minds the need for a change in the legal and political status of women in society. As Flexner puts it in *Century of Struggle*:

> Thousands of men and women were drawn into the work [of the Anti-Slavery Movement]; among the latter were the first conscious feminists, who would go to school in the struggle to free the slaves and, in the process, launch their own fight for equality. It was in the abolition movement that women first learned to organize, to hold public meetings, to conduct petition campaigns. As abolitionists they first won the right to speak in public, and began to evolve a philosophy of their place in

society and of their basic rights. For a quarter of a century the two movements, to
free the slave and liberate the woman, nourished and strengthened one another. (41)

During the Civil War in the United States, Mathilde Franziska Anneke
was in Switzerland, while her husband returned to America to fight for the
Union side. In Switzerland, she wrote many newspaper articles supporting
the North and several short stories portraying the humiliating and dehuman-
izing conditions of slavery. As could be expected, she was especially sensitive to the lot of women under this system, where their designation as
property made them fair game for lecherous owners. The dependent condition of women plus the debasing condition of slavery put a double burden on
black women, a burden that Anneke depicted in emotional terms in her stories. While today's readers might criticize a lack of distance or objectivity on
the part of the author, resulting sometimes in an almost overwhelming pathos, the strong emotional appeal was very effective with nineteenth-century
audiences. The reader has only to think of the impact of Harriet Beecher
Stowe's *Uncle Tom's Cabin* (1851) to be convinced of this.

Perhaps the best of her stories is "Die gebrochenen Ketten: Ein Bild aus
dem Süden der amerikanischen Union" ("Broken Chains: A Portrait from the
South of the American Union"). The full German text in modern script is
available in a collection of Anneke's works edited by Maria Wagner under
the title, *Die gebrochenen Ketten: Erzählungen, Reportagen und Reden
(1861–1873).*[2] My translation into English of the full text of the story follows.

Broken Chains: A Portrait from the American South

In the inner rooms of the beautiful Villa Magnolia in the southern part of the
District of Columbia there reigned a deep stillness, since in one of these bou-
doirs, provided with all the luxury of this country, the mistress of the place
rested in deep sleep. Heavy damask curtains hid the tall windows and let in
only the glimmer of a weak twilight. A sweet aroma, exuded by the exotic
bouquet of flowers held in the alabaster vase of a charming little forest god,
gave the air a heavy closeness.

The lady of the house, Lady Kingsbury, lay on snow-white pillows in her
slumber. At her feet knelt a young girl, who bowed her head and face into
her hands, a picture of the deepest sorrow for the woman who slumbered,

alas, too deeply, too still in the eternally long slumber of death. Death had led her into his dark shadowy kingdom and her departure was accompanied by touching love, thanks, and tears of suffering.

There was nothing more poor Lelia could do for her. She only wanted to place a white, hardly opened camellia with some green myrtle twigs on the breast of the dear departed,—for love had done everything which was in any way possible.

And yet, not everything. Her feeling rose like a wild tempest and over-powered her anxious heart. She fell on her knees and cried long and bitterly, and her cries of woe filled the rooms. It was a painful offering of tears and thanks, which the poor abandoned girl lay at the feet of the deceased.

Lelia was a slave. With her beloved mistress, the only friend of the poor girl, her refuge and protection, alas, her mother had departed this world.

If a funeral pyre had been lit, she would have considered herself fortu-nate to throw herself alive into its flames.

But she remained behind, alone and abandoned, without friends, without even a benevolent mistress. [What reasons (for self-immolation) did the fu-ture hide from the poor lovely girl!]

She was scarcely sixteen and had been a slave her entire lovely life long. But her slave's chains were a silken cord, woven with flowers, a knot which had never wounded her very sensitive feelings. She was treated by the good Lady Kingsbury like a child and in her house, where only goodness and love reigned, she was untouched by any raw wind which might blow outside.

Lady Kingsbury lived for many years as a widow. She had a son and a daughter, both of whom, since their marriages, lived in the capital of the Union, in Washington. She herself did not leave her beautiful villa and lived here, although alone, quite happily with servants who were devoted to her.

Her daughter, the proud Mrs. Randall, a southerner through and through, wife of Colonel Randall of a Virginia regiment, protested often about the way her mother spoiled her slaves and especially pampered her favorite Le-lia. The good child was continually a subject of their disagreements, and, no matter how charming and pretty she was considered, she was above all a born slave. This fact, according to the lady, should never for a moment be forgotten by a "respectable slaveholder." The mother only smiled at that, and while she was in no way deterred from her noble treatment, to the contrary, was even kinder to her little Lelia, she avoided any discussion of the matter with her hard-hearted daughter.

Because of that the good Lady Kingsbury was almost worshipped by her people. It was hardly necessary for her to express a wish, still less a command. Every task, even the smallest, was taken care of before she herself ever became aware of it.

Now death had called the good lady home. She lay ready to enter her eternal rest. Black funeral drapes veiled almost the whole of the large house of the former owner. However, deeper and darker than this was hidden in the hearts of all of her servants their grief at her departure. Into Lelia's many childlike feelings it crept with all her sufferings, and her only consolation was to mourn and weep for the dearest one she had in all the world. Alas, this consolation, too, was to be denied to her. A cutting whisper suddenly interrupted the deadly stillness of the funeral chamber and spoke her name in a sharp tone.

Shocked, she raised her head and glimpsed Mrs. Randall, who had just walked through the door to beckon to her. Lelia obeyed, following her mistress into the entrance hall and closing the door behind her.

Madame Randall, shocked, looked into the weeping face of the girl, and began nevertheless to show her long held-back resentment. There was in it unmistakably a certain amount of jealousy of the love which the dark-skinned girl had had for her mother; she even seemed angry at the grief through which this true heart expressed itself.

"Lelia," she said in a cold, haughty tone, "enough of that now; stop your crying and set about your work. You better believe, if you don't perform in a good orderly fashion, you'll be punished. I don't make pampered children of my servants, you'll see that soon enough. You've been spoiled and praised all too much, think yourself beautiful and better than your kind. There you are very much mistaken. In reality you are no better than the least of you; you are as much a slave as the blackest Negro woman in my house. You hear?"

Indeed poor Lelia had heard. She was too soon shocked out of her unending deep sorrow about the deceased and too quickly awakened into the knowledge that she—was a slave.

"Meta is in the dining room, busy with sewing the crepe border," continued Mrs. Randall, "go and help as much as possible; there are still over a hundred yards to make."

"Yes, Madame," Lelia answered, almost without knowing it, and hurried off.

"Why in such a hurry, you little apple of my eye," Mr. Allen Kingsbury called out, as he stepped into her way and threw his arm around her. "Mustn't be fearful."

Feverish blushing and trembling overtook poor Lelia; she turned her head and face away and struggled mightily to free herself. But Mr. Allen laughed triumphantly.

"Just don't be scared, little mouse!" he repeated. "You certainly are a sweet child, a little rascal. I wanna take you along to Washington and make you my lover. No one in the whole city will have a prettier one. From now on you belong to me, just so you know! You'll have it really good with me, don't need to work, wear the finest, prettiest clothes. You'd like that, now wouldn't you, Lelia? Come on now, look at me and call me your master."

Mr. Allen Kingsbury, son of the late Mrs. Kingsbury, was a man of about thirty-five. His appearance was proud and masterful. The severe line around his mouth indicated great force of will and rough egoism. In his eyes there was sensuality and a sharp look, which made clear that a victim once chosen was surely in his power.

Lelia had gotten free of his hands, she knew not how, and stumbled into the dining room. There sat Meta, the colored servant of Madame Randall. She sat at her work, crying.

"Come, help me, Lelia!" she called out impatiently. "Come quickly, otherwise the missus will punish me again. I work as hard as ever I can, but still she scolds me for being lazy. Oh, God!"

Lelia did not hide her affliction. With folded hands, she stood there, the very picture of despair. Oh, a slave—she, a slave? Never in her life had anyone dared to say this accursed word aloud about her; no one had ever called her that; it never occurred to her that the dark fate of slavery with all its terrors, all its grief and sorrow, rested upon her. Now it stood before her. A slave—a slave! She struggled as if in the agonies of torture.

The great dazzling mirror in the salon reflected the picture of her form and face, and she could have seen for herself how beautiful, how truly beautiful she was in her pain.

Her skin color, although somewhat dark olive, was clear and transparent; her full lips were red as cherry blossoms, her teeth like pearls were never lovelier, and her eyes were like stars. The dark veil of her hair, when loose, covered the most voluptuous forms and gave her curly locks the softest shadows.

Oh, unhappy beauty! If the most horrible fate, which earth's children must endure in this world, the fate of slavery, falls upon plain or ugly beings, it still calls forth pity, but when it strikes such dazzling loveliness, then it cries to heaven for a solution.

"A slave! And his slave!" screamed the unhappy victim. "Oh, can't I just die, can't I die?"

Meta, the dark-skinned Negro woman, looked up from her work amazed. She constantly had reason enough to complain of her terrible fate, which made her the property of a hard-hearted mistress, but the depth and the anguish which Lelia's tears and demeanor expressed, of such things she had no concept.

Lelia was quite clear about the character of Allen Kingsbury. She had often seen her dear departed mistress weep in silence about her son's conduct, and she had known quite well, what it meant when she tried to protect her from being seen by this man.

Poor girl! The innocence and womanly purity, which a motherly hand had sheltered and protected so truly, your only treasure should now be shamefully robbed from you.

"Allen Kingsbury's slave!" she repeated, wringing her hands; "completely in his power—oh, God have mercy!" She sank down to the carpet in tears.

"Get up this minute, and get to work!" scolded the voice of Mrs. Randall suddenly, trembling with emotion. "You're as bad as Meta, obey as little as she does. Get up, I say. If it weren't for my mother lying dead in this house, I would give you both a lesson you wouldn't forget!"

Lelia got up. She dried the tears from her eyes and with remarkably noble pride she began to work. Mrs. Randall stood for a while, watched the two girls with lowered heads and observed the great silence. Then she went into the parlor. There she found her brother, who immediately noticed her cloudy expression.

"What's wrong, dear Ludie?" Allen Kingsbury asked his sister. "You are unusually upset."

"Yes, that could well be. I get really annoyed with that worthless piece of work. Mother completely spoiled Lelia. I'm afraid I won't succeed in getting her in line, although my methods are tried and true and have never failed before, with even the most insolent creature."

"Oh, nonsense, leave the girl alone. She's alright; besides it's really quite unnecessary to worry and get all upset because I'm going to take her as part of my inheritance."

"Heaven forbid, Allen. Mother intended to give Lelia to me. With five months of proper training, she'll do well enough for me. She is a skilled seamstress, quite the most talented girl I've ever seen; worth more than six Metas, in my view. No, no, not another word about it. Lelia is my property."

"I'll take the liberty of one more word in reply, Madame," responded Mr. Allen Kingsbury. "Lelia is mine. I've desired her for two years, and you think, just because she's a nice girl, I would leave her to you?" The gentleman burst out in scornful laughter. "Oh, no, Madame Ludie Randall," he continued with tragicomic fervor: "She is probably much better off with me than with you. You'll treat her harshly and hard-heartedly, make her into an object of your training system. I will treat her like a queen. Take all the other rabble for yourself, but leave Lelia to me."

Mrs. Randall bit back a fit of rage. Although she did not say another word, she did not lose sight of her goal for a single moment. She just waited until the right moment came when the memory of her mother no longer required silence in those rooms, which had been blessed by her peaceful authority in life, to put right their existing differences. As long as the body of the deceased still lay on the bier, she wanted to at least observe proprieties, and not fight with her hot-tempered brother about what's mine and yours in her estate.

A long funeral procession of splendid carriages went through the gate of Villa Magnolia and accompanied the deceased to her last resting-place. Many tears and silent thanks for the constant kindness she had shown so many in life, followed her into the land of eternal peace. The loud laments and the despair of her servants here at her open grave were endless. They, the abandoned, helpless creatures, were the true mourners, children who were robbed of their mother, their benefactor, and their home, and they looked into their future, as dark, alas, as this melancholy grave.

Night had already fallen, and Lelia had stayed back alone at the grave, alone with the shadow of her beloved guardian. With a fierce suffering, which her Ethiopian feelings usually indulged without reservation, she finally left the mound around which her guardian spirit seemed to hover. When she arrived at the house, she was sick with grief.

The estate of the deceased was to be divided in half between the brother and sister. The mother had left the arrangement of this division to the two of

them. She knew that her son Allen was a gentleman in regard to things related to business and property, and undoubtedly took no special advantage
for himself in the case of a disagreement.

Nevertheless in this situation the poor slave girl became a bone of con-
tention between the two siblings. They would not let go in their fight over
possession of her.

"These are difficult times," Mr. Allen Kingsbury sighed. "Slave owner-
ship is becoming uncertain. The present war puts our blessed institution in
such a doubtful light that we shouldn't really squabble for a long time about
the questionable property. I want Lelia; the rest of the slaves which fall to my
half, I'll leave to you."

Mrs. Randall saw things the same way and for the same reason did not
want to do without Lelia.

Mr. Allen Kingsbury offered three times the worth of a normal slave, but
his sister would not agree under any circumstances. She stubbornly insisted
on making the lovely girl hers, and used all her energies against her equally
determined brother.

Meanwhile the discussion became more and more heated and was finally
not at all generous and brother- and sisterly. Bitter words were exchanged
and the end of the story was that there would be a public auction, and Lelia
would be put on the block with the rest of the slaves.

***

One evening most of the slaves at Villa Magnolia had assembled in the
kitchen, where Juno the cook had ruled with undisputed power for many
years. Juno was a respectable, rather nice-looking mulatto, although she was
past her prime. Along with her leadership skill, she possessed an extraordinary self-assurance, which made it possible for her to govern autocratically
and to exercise greater authority than her noble mistress had ever done in
life. She was a fine cook and prouder of this distinction than the former
leader of Louis XIV's multitudes, Vatel, honored all his life and certain of
victory. Besides, she had a good heart, in spite of her ill-tempered tongue.
She treated her "old man," who was a masterful coachman, like a little dependent child, while the only offspring, which heaven had sent her, was her
heart's adored idol.

Jane, the housemaid, and Alonzo, the manservant, sat on the steps that
led into the kitchen. Tears glistened in the eyes of both. They had been a
couple for a long time, and the late Lady Kingsbury had promised them that
they would soon be married. Lively Jane had thought about nothing but her

wedding for days and weeks, and about the white muslin dress, which the good lady had given her, decorated with lace and ribbons. Now all her hopes were gone, her entire happiness razed to the ground, and the hearts of the two lovers were full of bitter sorrow and deep suffering.

Nancy, the laundress, sat in the opposite corner and rocked a child next to her heart. Very dark in the face, she bore fully the darkest characteristics of her African race. She had not been a member of the Kingsbury household for long and had had little contact with her own kind. Her appearance was very sullen and repugnant so that noble Lady Kingsbury had often had to have patience with her unusual conduct. None of the other servants especially cared for her, but she too cared for no one except her little human creature which she held in her arms.

Poor Nancy! As sad and unfriendly as her fate, unloved—a slave—but still a woman—a mother.

She never spoke about her past life, and yet—she could have told the story of a tragedy! She had never known a homeland, never a human being who was devoted to her in friendship or in love. She was constantly passed from one slave handler to another, and her daily lot was work, misery, humiliation, and want. She had been a mother five times and each time, except for this last one, her child was torn from her heart in its most tender youth and alas—sold into slavery! She had struggled against this separation from her own flesh and blood with all her strength and fought like a tigress. After she was finally subdued, she fell into a dull, brooding despair. Her eyes had no more tears and her heart was as if turned into stone. There was only one soft spot within her where the word "mother" was written.

Juno's "old man" stood as if seeking shelter under his queen Baldachin on the hearth and gave a terrible sigh.

"If it must be, it must be," he began in the well-known English jargon that the blacks of the American South use. "Seems to me, it's hard on our parent hearts to separate from Jon, the good little boy. But Master Allen wants to take him, and Missus Randall takes us."

"Oh, my God!" Juno broke in. "It's all the same where we're supposed to be in the future, now that the old Missus has gone up to heaven. We'll never find a mistress like her again. Oh, my Lord God, how good she was! But Jon, alas, what hard times are coming for the poor boy. He is so headstrong and impertinent, poor, poor child!

At that very moment the youth sprang into the kitchen, over the heads of the couple who occupied the stairs, directly over, by placing the one hand on

Jane's left shoulder and the other on Alonzo's right. He was a slim, strong, brave-looking young man of fourteen with a dusky but light complexion. His expression was unusually intelligent and his features so purely European that he would hardly be taken for a born Southerner from America, still less for an Ethiopian, if not for his tight curly hair and his somewhat darker skin. To-day there was a very unusual expression on his face, his eyes shone so strangely, and his breathing came in great agitation.

"Mother, Mother!" he blurted out. "Tomorrow we are all going to be sold, all together at auction."

A cry of horror escaped all their lips.

"Oh, my Lord God, how can that be possible?" Juno moaned.

"Who told you, Jon?" Alonzo asked, getting up from his seat and standing in front of the little messenger of bad tidings.

"Master Jackson, just this very moment; he pets me on the head and says that I'm a cunning young man, and I'll see, tomorrow he'll buy me if the price doesn't go too high."

"Buy you? Oh, my Lord God!" Juno cried out and wrung her black, callused hands.

"Just what I said. Amazed, I asked him: buy me? Of course, he answered; your name, just like the names of the other slaves of your house, is on the list in the auction hall. We're to be sold tomorrow."

A murmur went through the groups, and the women broke out into the loudest lamentation.

Just at that moment, as Jon had spoken the last words of this bad news, Lelia made her way through the kitchen. She stood there as if made of stone. When she saw her, Jane, who had been sitting on the stairs up to this moment, got up.

"Yes, and you, you'll be sold as well," the latter hissed at her, with an expression that betrayed her, as if complete satisfaction for her own suffering could come to the unfortunate girl in her gloating over what was happening to the other. Jane was always somewhat jealous of Lelia's beauty and her preferential treatment. "Aha, now you also come to us, won't be more than all of us Negroes, aha!"

"Jane, Jane!" the good Alonzo exclaimed in a somewhat reproachful yet soothing tone.

"Then our mistress is dead, and the Day of Judgment is coming upon us all," Juno groaned. "My old man and I, we'll get through the world until we die, but—Jon, my Jon!" and all the horror of the greatly feared exile to the deep South appeared before the soul of the dark Moorish princess. "Oh, Jon will surely have to go to Georgia!" she exclaimed and began her lament anew with twice the strength.

"Mother, see here," the boy began to speak with almost authoritative tone. "I am a Negro,—but see, I never want to be a slave. I will wait for the moment when one day I can go over to Canada, the Promised Land."

As the boy spoke, he lifted his head proudly and showed in his whole being such a strong force of will that it was a pleasure to see the young Ethiopian. His mother, on the other hand, seemed too overwhelmed by thoughts of separation and had lost all of her boldness.

"Oh, don't do that," she begged; "don't do that, Jonnie. You'll be caught and then they'll whip you to death. Right, Nancy, you know?"

But Nancy was no longer conscious of anything. She sat there mute and passive, a sad figure, quietly absorbed within herself, her face hidden in the curly hair of her child. She had emitted aloud no sign of her grief, and the others had not concerned themselves with her in their own extreme suffering. No matter how quietly, how deeply the poor women seemed sunk in her pain, a last terrible despair arose in her dark, deranged feelings.

***

It was a frightful alternative for Lelia to be either the slave of Lady Randall or the slave of Mr. Allen Kingsbury. And yet, the decision had to be made. With quick steps, she flew into the chambers of the lady and, weeping and trembling in all her limbs, she threw herself on her knees at the lady's feet.

Mrs. Randall understood immediately the reason for Lelia's grief. She seemed unnerved in the first moment and turned visibly pale at the fleeting thought of inhuman, revolting injustice.

"Oh, Mrs. Randall, have mercy, have mercy!" Lelia pleaded.

"My God, what's wrong, child?"

"They say in the kitchen that we're all going to be sold tomorrow."

With a cold and indifferent expression, which Mrs. Randall had all too quickly taken on again, she answered with a short "yes, indeed!" However, her conscience soon seemed to try to lead her back, as her dying mother's last words beat urgently in her ears, to wit: Be good to my servants and especially accept my poor Lelia into your service.

"Oh, Mrs. Randall, I beg you on bended knee, keep me. I'll be good and hardworking, do everything in my power, willingly learn everything to make myself useful in your service, just don't throw me out, don't sell me. Let me work, let me suffer from hunger, beat me—but don't sell me."

"What a spectacle you're making," the lady said. "Aren't colored servants sold everyday? Is that worse for you than for the others?"

"No, certainly not, but my late mistress was so good, so loving to me, and I could never think that it was possible to be sold. Oh, God, sold, sold!" the poor girl moaned.

Mrs. Randall noticed that the pretty face, which earlier smiled so harmlessly, suddenly took on the characteristics of despair and madness. She sought as quickly as possible to defend herself from this impression, which was probably not quite comfortable for the lady, and said in a somewhat more subdued tone: "Now, now, child, be content. There's no way to avoid it. It really pains me, but it can't be changed. Consider, thousands of others, millions even, have the same fate. Now, be a good child, go and don't upset me any longer. I'm tired."

Lelia realized that her fate was sealed—and walked unsteadily away.

"Little, beloved Lelia! Don't cry," whispered Alan Kingsbury in her ear, as he stepped into her way as if by chance. Just as if the poisonous breath of a snake had touched her, she started suddenly. "You will be mine," he continued, "whatever Mrs. Randall may say. I have the same right as anyone else to buy you, isn't that so? You don't need to deck yourself out tomorrow for the auction. You can put on your worst dress, leave your hair uncombed, and look right stubborn and ill tempered. So much the better, the price will still go high enough. Now do what I told you, and bear in mind that I'm your future master."

The poor slave girl trembled in every limb; she could say nothing and only stammered a weak "yes." Then she fled—but, oh, God, where could she go with her affliction. She hardly knew any more.

The fearsome morning arrived. The walls in Villa Magnolia had never before seen such a quiet and sad group of people. The poor people had gathered in the kitchen to console each other in their suffering. They had to give up their home, in which, even though slaves, they were content and happy; they had to part from each other, they who had lived so well and peacefully with one another. Lelia had sneaked into a corner, no longer wearing a nice dress as was expected of her, no, wearing an outfit, dictated I don't know if by complete indifference, despair,—or the crude command of the "master."

Nancy still sat in the same place where they saw her yesterday, cowering motionlessly and dry-eyed, but her child still clasped in her arms.

"Hurrah! Hurrah! Yell hurrah with me and shoot off the cannons!" cried Jon boisterously, plunging into the kitchen with that one sentence, grabbing his mother, and forcing her to dance round and round with him as if crazy and delirious.

"Is the boy out of his mind?"

"Oh, no, no, shoot them off, I say, shoot them—Gloria, Gloria, Gloria!"

"Is the world ending, or what's wrong with him?" exclaimed Juno, gasping for breath.

"No, No!" cried the triumphant young man. "Only slavery is ending; we're free—we're all free!"

Those present stood in a circle around him; only Nancy stayed still in her place there in the corner. Little by little, to some extent excited by Jon's noisy behavior, they asked in broken sentences the meaning of his message.

The young man did not make them wait for a clearer explanation.

"Brother Brownson," he began, "was holding a sermon on the church steps, and all the Negroes were standing around him. Naturally, I ran over to hear the news. And what did he say?—He said: Shoot [off the cannons], Ethiopia, your chains have fallen. The day of your deliverance has come. You are free; you are free!"

Brother Brownson was a colored priest, loved and honored like a prophet among the unfortunate slaves of the entire region.

Imagine the awakening ray of hope, the sunshine upon the dark and despairing faces of those assembled in fear and terror. Imagine how they scarcely dared to breathe, and how they hung on every word of the young reporter as if it were a new gospel!

"Did the war do this?" asked Juno's old man.

"Oh, surely the Negroes finally revolted!" exclaimed Alonzo, and the youth's dark face flushed fire-red in the hopes that the long-awaited slave revolt had really broken out.

"Did the abolitionists come to free us?" asked a third, to which more and more questions followed in the next breath.

"No way!" Jon exclaimed. "It was a lot easier than you all think. The President in Washington did it himself."

"God bless him!" The words rang out as if from one mouth.

Then Jon continued with triumphant emotion: "He said: All Negroes in the District of Columbia are free! And when he says so, it's said and done. We won't be sold today, that's for sure—today we will be free. Hurray, hurray!" and Jon danced around the kitchen as if possessed. The others fell into each other's arms and cried for joy and happiness. Lelia trembled in surprise; she did not know whether she could rejoice and begged Jon to just stop dancing, and tell again what happened and what he really knows. The boy pulled a crumpled newspaper from the depths of his pocket and threw it to Lelia with the words: "There, you can read, read and tell me."

Far better informed than one of her kind, Lelia knew quite well what the war in which the country was currently involved might mean. She had regularly stayed up-to-date with the situation; she had constantly thought about the possibility and fed her hopes that the end of oppression for her poor brothers would come about.

She read and, her eyes shining, confirmed to those present everything Jon had reported. The slaves of the District of Columbia, that small speck of land, in whose center the White House shone in bright sunlight, and which, excluded from the states of the United States of America, was called only the District, [these slaves] are from this day forward free, and the slaveholders involved will be compensated. So states the proclamation of the President.

To freedom! Oh, what news! From the darkest night of slavery to the dawning of morning's freedom! Free, free! Blessed word to all people in whose ears it resounds as deliverance.

After the first outburst of joy among the colored friends had quieted down a little, a moment of relaxation and stillness. Was it really true what they heard, and not a dream? No, after all clever Lelia confirmed everything the boy had said, the whole, complete, so long-desired news. Since the message truly arrived at a moment of deepest hopelessness, the feelings of these unfortunate people had been so powerfully stirred up that they hardly could comprehend the truth. They alternated between silent doubt and wild demonstrations of joy.

Juno, who, as mistress of the kitchen, constantly moved with grave seriousness, had no doubts. Brother Brownson had proclaimed it, and Jon had heard it, that was enough to allow no hint of doubt to arise. She threw her powerful dark arm around the neck of her good husband and said simply: "Old man, may God be praised, we will not die as slaves."

"I've known that for a long time," Jon said in a saucy tone while marching around the kitchen with military stride and conducting himself like a young general. The pride of a newly freed man awoke in his breast. He never wanted to be a slave—in fact, chains would have been heavier for the poor rogue than for any other.

Alonzo and Jane fell into each other's arms and swore that, now that the chains of slavery were finally broken, they would willingly take upon themselves the sweeter chains of matrimony this very month.

Lelia's quiet triumph of deliverance was greater than all the others could imagine. One moment she, a slave, had lay in despair on the floor, groveling and whimpering in the dust before her tormentor. Now she stood straight, her chains had been loosened, [and] she could wrap herself in the cloak of innocence and womanhood and follow the path her noble foster-mother had taught her. Her heart rose as if carried on wings above to God, to praise him, to thank him. She left her partners in misery, now in joy, to their own demonstrations, which they presented in the characteristic manner of slaves, and rushed to the grave that would forever be dear to her. Here she sank down, and as if she wanted to press herself deeper and deeper against the buried remains, she hid her head in the lily wreaths with which the mound had been so richly decorated, and let her tears of thanks flow unhindered into the floral greens.

She was indeed free, no longer a slave! In the future, no one could say: look at me. I am your master! But she was an orphan, without a home, without friends. Where should she go in this wide, foreign world, in which she had only known Villa Magnolia? She called upon the spirit of her dear departed, and it seemed to her as if her soft voice could be heard in the morning breezes. Consoled and strengthened she rose to her feet.

Below, on the path in the park which led to the Villa, she met Allen Kingsbury. The great news of the day had affected him very much, one could see that clearly, and now, as he stood before Lelia, she seemed to almost overwhelm him. She stood immediately in front of him, but she was not afraid. She did not even tremble as she did yesterday when he said that she was to be his slave. Calmly and with womanly dignity, she raised her wonderful dark eyes and looked him freely and openly in the face. This look informed him fully that she knew he had no more power over her. He broke into a rage, gnashed his teeth, and waved his clenched fist in the air. Then he cursed the government and went on his way.

Madame Randall, along with her brother, had exhausted herself in her first outbursts of fury over the President's message. She sat pale and numb, a portrait of powerlessness. She was absorbed in thoughts about her future, when suddenly Juno stepped before her with outstretched arms and a very troubled look.

"Oh, Missus, Missus!" she cried. "What's happened with Nancy and her child! Oh, Nancy—Nancy, she's killed it."

Madame Randall was alarmed. She jumped up very quickly and followed the cook into the kitchen. There sat Nancy in the same unchanged position, in which people saw her since yesterday, a dark marble statue. Lelia bent over her and the child, who slept deeply and quietly in the sleep of death. The poor mother observed the small corpse with icy calm.

"Inhuman creature!" screamed Mrs. Randall. "She murdered it; yet people will have us believe that blacks have feelings just like whites. Here's proof."

"Indeed, strong proof!" replied a steady voice. "Because her feelings are stronger than yours, and her heart more self-sacrificing, she could see it go into a gentle death more calmly and blessedly in her arms than into cursed slavery."

Was that Lelia, the small fearful girl, who spoke in this sure and calm tone? The same girl who yesterday lay at the feet of the lady and gasped for breath and begged that she might be, not a queen, not a beloved child, that she might be nothing more than a slave—her slave?

Accusing spirits arose before the frightened conscience of Madame Randall. The dead child, the mother paralyzed in the death struggle, the avenging girl with her voice of justice and sadness,—it was all too much for her guilt-laden feelings. Slowly, without saying a word, she turned and stole away.

"Poor Nancy," cried the girl, "now we are free and your child—." Tears choked her voice.

"Free?" stammered the poor woman without comprehending the meaning of the word, and looking with wide-opened eyes into the gentle face of pity. Death also breaks chains. Freedom on this earth came to her too late.

With the shine of the last spark of a true mother's love, she pressed her dead baby once more frantically to her heart and then sank back into eternal deliverance in the arms of a free and pure maiden.

The girl kissed her on the forehead and lay her down gently, the tiny child at her side.

[End of Anneke's text]

With an excellent understanding of her nineteenth-century audience, Mathilde Anneke was able to weave a human tragedy to illustrate the abuses of slavery. While she was equally capable of writing an essay or a powerful speech to make her points, the use of a short story was also an effective vehicle for her. She could detail the causes of individual suffering by imagining the consequences of the lack of freedom. Women such as Lelia and Nancy were especially vulnerable: the attractive young woman to the predation of the master of the house or his sons, the mother to having her children condemned to a life of slavery, even sold off to another family and separated from her. Having painted the intolerable picture of slavery through a specific example, Anneke was also able to use the power of fiction to dramatize the precious moment of freedom. For the young mother, freedom came only through death, but for Lelia and the others, the ending of the story holds hope for a better life in this world. As Anneke saw parallels between slavery and the legal condition of dependence forced upon women, her ending with the freeing of slaves also contains her hope that women's legal condition might also change. After all, her women characters clearly carry a double burden because of their position in society as women and as slaves. Historically, Anneke believed that change—as was the case with the abolition of slavery—was inevitable (see Chapter 6).

It is against this background that Anneke's stand with Susan B. Anthony and Elizabeth Cady Stanton against the Fifteenth Amendment should be understood. She was not opposed to the franchise for newly freed slaves, but rather was opposed to enfranchising only former male slaves and excluding all women. She agreed with Stanton's opinion on the question when she wrote for the *Revolution* October 21, 1869 (cited in *The History of Woman Suffrage*, vol. 2, 333–334 by Frost & Cullen-DuPont 202):

All wise women should oppose the Fifteenth Amendment for two reasons:

1. Because it is invidious to their sex. Look at it from what point you will, and in every aspect, it reflects the old idea of woman's inferiority, her subject condition. And yet the one need to secure an onward step in civilization is a new dignity and self-respect in women themselves. No one can think that the pending proposition of 'manhood suffrage' exalts woman, either in her own eyes or those of the man by her side, but it does degrade her practically and theoretically, just as black men were more degraded when all other men were enfranchised.

2. We should oppose the measure, because men have no right to pass it without our consent. When it is proposed to change the constitution or fundamental law of the State or Nation, all the people have a right to say what that change shall be.

If women understood this pending proposition in all its bearings, theoretically and practically, there would be an overwhelming vote against the admission of another man to the ruling power of this nation, until they themselves were first enfranchised. There is no true patriotism, no true nobility in tamely and silently submitting to this insult. It is mere sycophancy to man; it is licking the hand that forges a new chain for our degradation; it is indorsing the old idea that woman's divinely ordained position is at man's feet, and not on an even platform by his side.

By this edict of the liberal party, the women of this Republic are now to touch the lowest depths of their political degradation.

During the Civil War, as has been mentioned, Mathilde Franziska Anneke focused much of her writing while in Switzerland on the horrors of slavery, but she never ceased fighting for women's rights as well and often combined arguments for improving the lot of both. When the slaves were finally free, and the Civil War ended, Anneke returned to Wisconsin and focused her considerable talent and energy on a final project she felt would improve the lives of young women. She took progressive ideas about women's education and applied them to her own school.

Notes

1. See, for example, Flexner 70–72.
2. The Wisconsin Historical Society has in its archives a nineteenth-century copy of this work, *Die gebrochenen Ketten: Ein Sitten-Gemälde nach Quellen aus dem Süden bearbeitet von Mathilda Franziska Anneke, geb. Giesler*. It appears in the *Sonntags-Blatt Herold*, No. 101. Milwaukee, from Saturday, July 9, 1864, and No. 102, from Saturday, July 23, 1864 (Box 6 Folder 9 WisMssLW).

Chapter 8

Education for Women

Education became an issue for nineteenth-century women reformers because of the great disparity in the type of education received by boys and girls. This was true in Germany, as it was in the United States. Before Mathilde Franziska Anneke left for America after the failure of the Revolution of 1848, she criticized several aspects of the German education system in her newspaper editorials, especially the role of the church in controlling education (see Chapter 2). From the practical point of view, Anneke argued that education was outside of the area of church competence, and that skills such as reading, writing, and arithmetic have no need to be taught from a Christian viewpoint. As a political activist, she believed church control kept women and children from using reason to form their own independent opinions. However, from the structural point of view, this was the system in which she grew up and the one with which she would have been most familiar. She would also have been influenced by contemporary ideas of reform in curriculum and teaching methodology.

According to German law, both boys and girls were to receive a state education up to the age of fourteen, according to the Stern/Hardenberg reforms in Prussia in 1807 (Diethe 2), but girls were usually tutored at home. Fanny Lewald, for example, describes her education in her autobiography,[1] and it was not atypical for a young woman of her class. However, her education was clearly geared toward making her an accomplished wife, not toward preparing her for a profession outside of the home. Boys' schools educated them for the *Abitur*, the exam required for university entrance. Girls could certainly prepare at home through private tutors, but German universities did not accept them as regular students until after 1900, as opposed to as auditors who were allowed to sit in at some universities at an earlier date. A state primary education was part of the laws of the German Reich in 1871, but the provision of a full thirteen years of schooling (until age 19) was not part of the law until 1908 (Diethe 2). Until the latter part of the nineteenth century, German women were not allowed to pursue a university degree in Germany; however, some did study outside of Germany in the Swiss universities of Zurich and Bern. When Luise Büchner traveled to Zurich in 1875, she was impressed and very encouraged to see men and women studying side by side, all of which she described in "Eine Reise-Erinnerung" (1875: "A Travel Memoir"; Dierks 221–236).

Well-known nineteenth-century German writers on education for women were very much influenced by a belief in separate spheres for men and women. That belief naturally had an impact on the type of education they favored for women. Jean Paul Richter (1763–1825), while sympathizing with woman's position in society, nevertheless emphasized that her most important work was the raising of children. He criticized a "showy education" for women, one in which "formal accomplishments" (Woody 79–80) were stressed. Instead, he saw the importance of an education for women because of her role within the family as wife and mother. Karl von Raumer wrote in a similar vein in his *Education for Girls* (1861). He recommended "intellectual cultivation," including the study of reading, writing, French, English, arithmetic, singing, piano, drawing, botany, and some history, because not to engage their intellect would cause girls' minds to turn to foolish and idle pursuits. However, he also included the necessity of learning "dexterity with needle and thread, knitting, and other housewifely employments" so that they would be able to contribute successfully to the household (Woody 80–81). As Woody notes in his book, *A History of Women's Education in the United States*, a woman's education was seen "from the standpoint of social needs rather than individual desire. He [Raumer] began and ended with the family and her place in it. The improvement of society, so ardently sought after by many through reforms of state or church, he held, could only be achieved by putting at its basis the healthy family life…" (81). The reawakening of interest in girls' education at the end of the seventeenth century, and even more evident in the middle of the eighteenth century, including the establishment of *Töchterschulen*, was still very much focused on the expected improvement in home life that might result. Toward the end of the nineteenth century, changes occurred in the public secondary education of girls that would lead to the admission of women to universities.

Many German women writers of the nineteenth century wrote and spoke in favor of more educational opportunities for women. Within Germany, groups such as the Lette-Verein (1860s), the Allgemeiner Deutscher Frauen-verein (1865 in Leipzig), and the Frauen Bildung-Reform-Verein (1888 in Weimar) among others (Woody 85), strove to improve higher-education fa-cilities for women. Education and emancipation were seen as complemen-tary; yet along with a desire for better education, there was also a fear of ridicule if a woman became "too learned." The view that men and women occupied different spheres in society was still accepted by most nineteenth-century reformers. In Germany, Luise Büchner speaks for many women of her time and social class through her essay "Die Frauen und ihr Beruf" ("Women and Their Vocation"), in which she argues for the value of woman's role in society, and for the necessity of a carefully planned educa-tion to enable her to fulfill her role effectively. The discussion by the mid-nineteenth century was thus most often framed in terms of what type of edu-cation was appropriate for women, no longer whether women should have an education or not.

Societal attitudes toward women and education continued to have a tre-mendous influence on the women themselves, even as they saw deficiencies in their own education, which influenced their position in society. Many nineteenth-century women writers accepted Rousseau's description of them as a "repository of moral rectitude, close to nature and the emotions and therefore able to guide rational man in matters of the heart" (Diethe 7). This view appears in his *Julie, ou la nouvelle Héloise* (1761), and was so well known that when Luise Büchner referred simply to Julie in her essay "Die Frauen und ihr Beruf," she was so sure her readers would understand the ref-erence that she made no further explanation than the mention of the name. This character stood as an obvious ideal for the women Büchner was ad-dressing.

The Enlightenment ideal of the morally pure wife was embraced in the nineteenth century where "marriage of convenience" was the norm. Material well-being was difficult or impossible for a woman to achieve through her own work, especially in the early nineteenth century, and marriage was often described as a woman's natural "career." When a marriage of convenience was unhappy and ended in divorce, the woman was almost certain to suffer material want. Louise Aston, for example, referred to in Anneke's famous essay "Woman in Conflict with Society" (see Chapter 3) received only a small stipend from the courts for herself and her daughter, but her ex-husband did not pay even that small sum regularly. Her writing became her way of earning their living. Because education was such a crucial factor in preparing to pursue a career, the fight for women's education paralleled their fight for improvement in their legal standing, and for their acceptance in the professions. Among women writers of the nobility and the bourgeoisie, these issues were central to the whole question of emancipation, which continued into the twentieth century.

Historian Gerda Lerner discusses the development of education for women in her books *The Creation of Feminist Consciousness* and *The Majority Finds Its Past*. As she writes in her introduction to the second of these, nineteenth-century women were not illiterate, but their education usually included only an elementary education, and much of that was accomplished at home (11). In the United States, during the colonial period and on the frontier, division of labor occurred but did not imply a lower status for women. However, the critical period occurred when educational opportunities became available to some and not to others. Lerner writes in *The Majority Finds Its Past*: "when education began to be institutionalized, the exclusion of girls from higher education was an actual deprivation and implied lower status. Similarly, the access to a variety of occupations enjoyed earlier by colonial women became limited as soon as American society had advanced to a point where professionalization could take place" (51). Exclusion from such professional fields as law and medicine because higher education was not available to them meant fewer opportunities for women in the early nineteenth century. Lerner points out that historical change "gave rise to a sense of status displacement in an educated, white, middle-class elite, and that led to the emergence of the organized woman's rights movement" (52). It is interesting to note, however, that the professionalization of teaching during the period 1820–1860 brought many additional women into that field (23). As public education expanded, and the number of schools increased, the cost of providing teachers became a consideration. Women were hired in greater numbers because they worked for less than men did; Lerner notes that 30–50 percent of male wages was considered the proper "wage differential" (24).

The "educational disadvantaging of women," as Lerner so tellingly refers to it in her book *The Creation of Feminist Consciousness*, was observed by women from educated families on both sides of the Atlantic. Many of the women who criticized this state of affairs did not plan to challenge women's role in society. Women such as Luise Büchner in Germany, as well as pioneers in women's education in the United States such as Mary Lyon, Catharine Beecher, and Emma Willard spoke of the importance of women's work, especially in raising and educating children, and believed that education was central to maintaining the dignity and status of what was clearly an essential contribution made to society by women. Emma Willard (1787–1870) advanced the concept of "republican motherhood," in which she argued that women, as mothers, form the character of the future citizens of the democracy, and therefore needed to have their own character well formed through education (Lerner *Feminist Consciousness* 215). The schools established by Lyon, Beecher, and Willard, as well as the private school Mathilde Franziska Anneke founded, were intended to offer curricula equal to what was offered in men's schools. The purpose of the early American pioneers was to provide teachers for the new public schools, and as Lerner notes, they were very successful. She also notes the unexpected consequence that "the existence of so many graduates with better educational qualifications led to an ever-increasing demand by women for access to colleges and universities" (*Feminist Consciousness* 43). I should note that Anneke was not as conservative in her views as these early women pioneers in regard to education or a "woman's sphere." Her experiences and participation in the Revolution of 1848 left her with a firm belief in the equality of men and women, and the conviction that women should be able to pursue whatever career they chose. She was therefore fully in support of higher education for women. As Maria Wagner clearly indicates, Anneke's own girls' school (Madam Anneke's German–French–English Academy), founded in 1865, was based on the German *Gymnasium*, which served to prepare students planning to attend the university ("A German Writer and Feminist" 166–167).

Writing in 1947 in the United States, Eleanor Wolf Thompson examined ideas on education from the mid-nineteenth century in her book, *Education for the Ladies 1830–1860: Ideas on Education in Magazines for Women*. In defending her choice of time period, she explained:

> The period 1830–1860 was one of reform and humanitarianism. The Maine Law spurred temperance workers in every state to greater and ever hopeful activity; the Fugitive Slave Law, the Kansas-Nebraska Act and the Dred Scott decision fired the opponents of slavery with zeal; the Women's Rights Convention at Seneca Falls in 1848 initiated the formal and conscious effort for women's rights. All these reformers and others, including those for whom education was "The Cause," recognized the need for education. It was a period, too, when women were demanding a reconsideration of their status and of the range of their activities and were seeking a place

in public affairs. It was a period of far reaching educational developments, as the rise of the common school, the growth of public high schools for girls as well as boys, the development of normal schools, the establishment of colleges in every section of the country and even of coeducational colleges and colleges for women. There were educational experiments, inspired both by European and American educators, and by the belief that education was a great democratizing force. Education was of vital interest to the people of the mid-nineteenth century and the popular periodicals reflected this interest." (vi–vii)

Fresh from her revolutionary experiences in Germany, Mathilde Anneke entered the United States at the height of this period of reform, with her political attitudes in sympathy with the desired changes, and hope for a democratic environment not found in her native land. Hers was not a unique experience. It was during this period that a wave of German refugees, called the Forty-Eighters, immigrated to the United States in the aftermath of the failed Revolution of 1848. Members of the increasingly political teachers' movement of that period were well represented among the Forty-Eighters. Indeed, some became quite active in reform movements when faced with political corruption, slavery and racism, American nativism, and the influential position of the Protestant churches, with their strong impetus in the American Temperance Movement (Goldberg 203–206). As Bettina Goldberg points out in her article on the impact of the Forty-Eighters on the U.S. school system, "The Forty-Eighters in America: The Theory and Practice of Reform," one characteristic of this group of immigrants was the "conviction, originating in the idealistic philosophy of the Enlightenment, that education was a means of effecting change in society" (207). Some of the ideas that Anneke and others had supported in Germany, such as the separation of Church and school functions, free elementary education, and the teaching of science, were already part of the system in the United States, but the Forty-Eighters criticized the methodology. Citing contemporary sources, including an article in the *Erziehungs-Blätter*, Goldberg lists these defects: "pupils did not learn how to learn and think but only to memorize facts; the teaching method did not take the age of children into account or include any visual and practical elements but was generally abstract and concentrated on the repetition of definitions which the pupils had not even understood; lively discussion between teacher and pupils was not central to teaching, but rather reading and learning by rote from textbooks; and, finally, absolutely no attention was paid to developing the children's artistic and physical capabilities through singing, drawing, and gymnastics" (207). The teaching of practical subjects was frequently mentioned in ladies' magazines in their discussion of curricula. The two subjects most often mentioned in this regard were "domestic economy" and physical education (Thompson 48). The skills necessary for running an efficient household were often looked at as a type of practical science and were expected to be taught as such (Thompson 49–50; also a repeated idea in Luise Büchner). However, outstanding women's academies, while enlarging the range of subjects, especially in the sciences (for example, chemistry, physics, botany, and geology), generally did not give courses in "housewifery or domestic science" (Solomon 23). Their focus on the practical involved the sciences along with such fields as rhetoric, mathematics, and geography. Meanwhile, physical education, sometimes called calisthenics, was valued because the healthy body and healthy mind were to be developed together. Once again, women's magazines would often connect physical activity with the practical purpose of making women better wives and mothers, strong and capable of raising their children and performing the necessary work of running a household.

Public opinion in favor of women's education was clearly tied to the question of its utility. The arguments using the ideal of "republican motherhood" reasoned that women needed to be educated to raise citizens for a democratic nation. In the nineteenth century, the ideal of the Christian wife, mother, and teacher also contributed to the perceived need for women's education. As Solomon notes in her book *In the Company of Educated Women: A History of Women and Higher Education in America*, when women's influence was considered crucial in families and communities, "republican and Christian rationales made a formidable combination justifying the education of women" (15–16). Educating women as teachers became an extension of their role within the family and was considered an appropriate career. The public purposes for women's education were, however, only part of the growing rationale. Families with unmarried daughters could readily see the advantage in educating these daughters to be teachers and earn a salary to support themselves in the event they did not marry (Solomon 16). In New England, innovators such as Emma Willard, Catharine Beecher, Zilpah Grant, and Mary Lyon, although accepting some of the constraints placed on the women of their time, were achievers in their own communities and had themselves struggled to obtain higher education (Solomon 17). They believed firmly in the academic advancement of their women students, and the curriculum offered in the women's academies began to reflect the accepted curriculum at male academies.

Nevertheless, another weakness often criticized in the schools was the lack of qualified teachers. Goldberg cites Rudolf Dulon's opinion that it was "regrettable that primarily women were employed as teachers in order to save costs, even though it had been established that the female sex was unsuitable for the teaching profession" (Goldberg 207). His attitude reflects the common conservative attitude of male Forty-Eighters in regard to the position of women in society and the assumption that women were intellectually inferior. Women Forty-Eighters such as Mathilde Franziska Anneke fought repeatedly against this traditional attitude in regard to education, as well as when they tried to obtain support for women's voting rights from their usually liberal-minded compatriots within the German-American community. Interestingly, the idea that women teachers lowered the academic level of schools continued to be expressed throughout the second part of the nineteenth century. The Report of the International Council of Women, March 25–April 1, 1888, assembled by the National Woman Suffrage Association[2], reports the discussion of the role of women as educators as part of a review of the advances in women's education. In the proceedings, Susan B. Anthony mentions that President Elliott of Harvard University attributed the deterioration of the public schools to the fact that there were too many women teaching. She then adds that she wishes Professor Rena A. Michaels, an accomplished and articulate woman in the field of education (dean of Northwestern University and reporting at the conference on "Women as Educators" 165–167) could have been present in order to rebut his statement decisively in public.

In Milwaukee, where Anneke would found her own school, dissatisfaction with the existing school system was the reason for the establishment of private schools (Goldberg 209–210). Education reformers such as Fröbel and Pestalozzi were well known in Germany, and their ideas drove an interest in education to develop independent thinkers. While Thompson notes that German women's magazines advocated German schools as a way to preserve German language and culture (54, 64), and surely this was a consideration, the Forty-Eighters in Milwaukee were especially critical of what they saw as an unacceptable choice in schools: either private German Lutheran or Catholic schools where the instruction was only in German, or poorly equipped and crowded public schools with no German instruction (Goldberg 210). Based on their political convictions, the liberal Forty-Eighters rejected schooling with religious affiliation and instead "established their own schools based on principles of secularism, bilingualism, and practical orientation" (Goldberg 210). Mathilde Franziska Anneke's school was founded exactly along those lines.

Education of women in Milwaukee was strongly associated with Catharine E. Beecher (1800–1878). A preeminent figure in nineteenth-century women's education, she devoted some fifty years to various educational projects. She opened a seminary in Hartford in 1828 at the beginning of her career, and her *Educational Reminiscences,* looking back on her career, were published in 1874 (Woody 319). In between she wrote prolifically and did the practical work of education. Beecher was strongly committed to giving her students the necessary knowledge and skills "to prepare the young for the active duties of life and to enable them to fill with propriety the stations to which, by Providence, they may be called…" (cited in Woody 318). However, politically she opposed suffrage as a burden that women were not ready to take on. She argued in her 1872 book *Woman's Profession as Mother and Educator* that the evils of society should be remedied by changing oppressive laws and asking directly for what was needed instead of asking for the ballot (17–18). As an educator, she advocated a comprehensive and practical educational program with a strong religious purpose (Woody 318). Beecher was especially interested in the education of teachers. In addition to her work in Hartford, she had worked in Cincinnati, Ohio; Burlington, Iowa; and Quincy, Illinois. Thus her influence was well accepted before she was invited to establish a school in Milwaukee (1852), the Milwaukee Normal Institute and High School, later called Milwaukee Female College (Woody 325).

Anneke's school, therefore, was founded in an environment where there was already considerable interest in the education of women. Her Milwaukee Töchter-Institut offered a well-rounded education including mathematics and science to her women students, who comprised both day students and boarders (Blackwell 3). In contrast to Beecher's approach to education, Anneke preferred to follow the tradition of the Forty-Eighters of separating the educational system from any religious purpose.

Anneke's interest in education dates from her years in Germany when she criticized church control of schools in her *Frauen-Zeitung.* The idea of founding a school was one she had entertained for a long time. In her letter from Paris to her sister Johanna Weißkirch, dated March 30, 1865, Mathilde Anneke writes of her plans to act on this idea upon her return to the United States (Wagner, *MFA in Selbstzeugnissen* 217): "Ich wünsche mich selbständig in einer Stadt niederzulassen, in der ich vereint mit Cäcilie Kapp arbeiten und meine Existenz sichern kann." ("I want to settle independently in a city where I can work with Cäcilie Kapp and earn a secure living.") Her later references make it clear that she plans to set up a school, if at all possible in Milwaukee. Although Anneke weighs the possibility of remaining in Europe and earning her living through journalism, she decides to return with her children to their homeland, rather than impose on them the type of rootlessness she experiences. She calls this burden the "Fluch der Heimatslogkeit" ("the curse of homelessness," used in the sense that she has lost the feeling of belonging in her homeland [*Heimat*]). Her family ties bring her back: "ich kehre zurück, weil ich dort meine lieben Lebenden und meine unvergeßlichen Toten habe" ("I am returning because I have my beloved family [those living] and my unforgettable deceased [children] there."). However, she has no interest in moving to St. Louis where her husband, Fritz, has relocated, as she tells him in her letter of June 13, 1865 from Paris (Wagner, *MFA in Selbstzeugnissen* 222–224). The climate would aggravate her illness, and she mentions her lack of interest in the "old slave state of Missouri" with the words: "Dann reizt mich der alte Sklavenstaat Missouri auch nicht*." While her personal preference would be to make a new home in or near New York, her ailing mother is in Milwaukee, and her sister Johanna is there to look into the necessary preparations for opening a school. At the end of her letter to her sister (March 30, 1865; Wagner, *MFA in Selbstzeugnissen* 219), she asks her to find out some basic information for her: what might be the prospects for a school for the daughters of German and English families; whether it would be better to found a day school or a boarding school; if the French language should be emphasized; and finally, whether Cäcilie should join an already established American academy. All these questions help Anneke to research the probabilities of success for her idea. Once she weighed all the factors, Anneke chose Milwaukee as at least the first "station" in her new American life (Wagner, *MFA in Selbstzeugnissen* 223). Her project was certainly not an easy one, but with considerable planning and work she was quite successful, with the result that she remained for the rest of her life in Milwaukee.

The school was the focus of her plans to earn a living. Anneke makes clear in her letter to her husband that she is beginning a new chapter in her life, and she wants meaningful work to be an important part of it. She writes in her June 13, 1865 letter: "Ich sehne mich jetzt unaussprechlich nach einer geeigneten und lohnenden Tätigkeit." ("I now have this inexpressibly strong desire for an appropriate paid position.") She has come out of her war years in Europe, where money was often scarce, and now wishes to settle down with an established career and home. While Fritz was certainly welcome to join the family in Milwaukee, she was not willing to start over in St. Louis, which in her view was much less favorable to her enterprise. In addition to being a place Mathilde Anneke was familiar with, and where her mother was living, Milwaukee in the nineteenth century was also a center for German immigrants (Wagner, *MFA in Selbstzeugnissen* 232), and here she found a place for herself in the environment of German customs and German language. Her own mastery of English was never as strong as she would have wished, and in this community she was known and admired, as Blackwell notes in her 1995 article (describing Anneke as an early feminist), even if few who sent their daughters to her school shared her views on Woman Suffrage (3). Anneke herself was aware that her views might seem too radical for the conservative environment of the city.

Her joint venture with Cäcilie Kapp is described in the letter of March 30, 1865, to her sister. She would leave the establishment of the Lady's Academy to Cäcilie and contribute her own work and talents wherever she could be of use. She clearly plans to promote the Academy and obtain the necessary funding for its success. She also intends to continue her literary work and see to the education and future of her children, Percy and Hertha. As an experienced educator, Cäcilie Kapp seems more suitable to run the Academy. Anneke writes: "Cäcilie hat die gediegensten Kenntnisse. Sie spricht nicht nur alle drei Sprachen: English, Französisch, Deutsch sehr fließend, sondern versteht auch Italienisch, spielt Klavier, kurz, ist eine bedeutende Erscheinung und, was das meiste: eine erfahrene Pädagogin, auf welche Requisition man in Milwaukee schon stolz sein könnte. Warum ich bei dem Unternehmen im Hintergrund bleiben möchte, ist, weil vielleicht meine radikalen Ansichten nicht förderlich erscheinen dürften, Cäcilie aber praktisch und klug genug ist, den gemäßigten Weg einzuschlagen. Sie ist keineswegs wie ich eine Heidin, vielmehr ziemlich religiös, doch so, daß es mich in unserem Freundschaftsverkehr nicht unangenehm berührt" (Wagner, *MFA in Selbstzeugnissen* 217–218) ("Cäcilie has the most appropriate knowledge. She not only speaks all three languages, English, French, and German, very fluently, but she also understands Italian, plays piano, in short is an accomplished individual. And what's more she is an experienced educator, whom people could be very proud to have in Milwaukee. The reason I would like to stay in the background in this venture is that my radical views would probably not be beneficial. However, Cäcilie is practical and smart enough to take a moderate approach. She is not at all a heathen like me; on the contrary [she is] rather religious, but in such a way that it does not make me uncomfortable in our relationship as friends.")

While Cäcilie Kapp had the necessary background and experience for the academic side of their venture, including experience in Switzerland with her parents' boarding school (Wagner, *MFA in Selbstzeugnissen* 245), Anneke attended to many of the practical aspects of their school, the running of the household and provision of meals. She was thrifty and with careful use of their funds able to make a financial success of the school, although not without periods of financial strain, during which she earned additional money through lectures, private classes, and writing (Wagner, *MFA in Selbstzeugnissen* 248). In 1869, Kapp left the school to take a position at Vassar College. However, she retained contact with Anneke throughout her life and supported the school by work during her vacations and even sometimes with financial help (Wagner, *MFA in Selbstzeugnissen* 245). The school gained prestige, particularly for the effective teaching methods Anneke applied and the excellent teachers she was able to employ.

Beyond her role as school director, Anneke herself taught classes. In an 1868 letter, she mentions her preparations for history, literature, geography, mythology, and rhetoric (Wagner, *MFA in Selbstzeugnissen* 270) along with her work in hiring for other areas. An ad for her school stresses a practical education where American and German girls would study in an appropriate yet comfortable environment. The aim was for a homelike atmosphere with interesting coursework taught by Anneke herself and outstanding teachers. Her ad for the Milwaukee Töchter-Institut mentions specifically as areas of study: German and English language including grammar, essay writing, literature and conversation; the French language; world and cultural history; the fields of geography, natural science and arithmetic; drawing, music, and rhetoric; and finally women's handiwork (Wagner, *MFA in Selbstzeugnissen* 247). In the spring of 1868, she was able to move her school into a house on Jefferson Street, which she describes enthusiastically as "elegant and delightfully well located" (Wagner, *MFA in Selbstzeugnissen* 267). From later student testimonials, it is apparent that Anneke's own love of learning and her interest in effective teaching methodology enabled her to make learning enjoyable for her students (304–308). Her influence over the direction of their lives is mentioned by several of her former students. The reputation of her school spread well beyond Milwaukee and attracted students from other parts of the United States (303–304).

Mary Wright Sewall's report on the state of higher education to the International Council of Women in 1888, just after Mathilde Anneke's death, places Anneke's accomplishments in the context of her time. As Sewall traces the genesis and growth of education for women, she traces the progression from boarding schools to female seminaries to co-educational academies to female colleges. Anneke's Töchter-Institut, with a curriculum similar to that in boys' academies, was both a boarding school and a type of female seminary. With her more advanced curriculum, she clearly hoped her students might be prepared to go on to higher education. Her activities toward the end of her life focused on the direction of further education for women. For example, she participated in the 1874 Detroit Convention of the National German-American Teacher's Association where she joined others[3] in pushing to create a German-American College. This effort was successful with the opening of the National German-American Teachers' Seminary in 1879 in Milwaukee (Tolzmann 275). In addition, Sewall's report refers to what she calls "irregular" means of educating women, such as clubs, lectures, and correspondence societies (National Woman Suffrage Association 53). Anneke also participated in that type of education through her lectures on German literature. One example appears in a letter to Fritz Anneke from March 1869 where she refers to an open lecture on "Nibelungen: Uranfänge deutscher Dichtkunst" ("Nibelungs: The Earliest Origins of German Literature"), for which she received a much-needed payment of one-hundred dollars (Wagner, *MFA in Selbstzeugnissen* 277).

In assessing Anneke's school, parents of some of the students refer to it as "one of the best institutes in the Northwest" and cite the excellent education and treatment their daughters received. They even note that the principles of the women's convention in New York are Anneke's private convictions and are not brought into the materials taught, in case parents should fear having their daughters adopt such opinions. Interestingly, both they and the former students stress that Anneke always showed an openness and strength of character, which they admired (Wagner, *MFA in Selbstzeugnissen* 304). The development of independent thinking and character seems to have been an important part of what Anneke achieved with her students. A former student writes eloquently: "And the knowledge which we gained was in fact the least of what we took with us from her classes. Our whole being was filled with all that is beautiful, noble, pure [and] good. We were better people because we had spent time with her. She impressed upon us the imprint of her beautiful soul. Whoever followed her efforts needed no other religion. To emulate her, a person had to reach for the stars."[4] The student goes so far as to write that Anneke's students stood out in that, whatever difficulties they encountered in life, they always maintained the highest ideals, a striving for what is moral, and an ethical inner compass that directed their lives toward their duty. She was, for them, on the level of a *Priesterin* (priestess).[5] Indeed, the impact Mathilde Anneke had on some of her students, as they moved beyond a woman's sphere as defined at the beginning of the nineteenth century, should certainly be counted as an important part of her legacy.

NOTES

1. Available in translation as *The Education of Fanny Lewald: An Autobiography.* Translated by Hanna Ballin Lewis (Albany: State University of New York Press, 1992).

2. Available in the Susan B. Anthony Collection of the Library of Congress, Washington, DC.

3. Tolzmann refers specifically to Adolf Douai and Heinrich H. Fick. His article (273–284) focuses on Fick's contributions to the teaching profession. He was a leader in the creation and direction of the seminary, and was a member of the administrative board for forty years until the college closed in 1918 (due to the anti-German feelings generated by World War I).

4. *MFA in Selbstzeugnissen* 307. The text reads: "Und die Kenntnisse, die wir uns erwarben, waren doch noch das Geringste, was wir aus ihren Stunden mitnahmen. Unser ganzes Ich war durchdrungen von dem Schönen, dem Edlen, dem Reinen, dem Guten. Wir waren bessere Menschen, indem wir in ihrer Nähe geweilt hatten. Sie prägte uns den Stempel ihrer schönen Seele auf. Wer ihrem Streben folgte, bedurfte keiner anderen Religion. Ihr nachzueifern mußte man nach den Sternen zielen."

5. *MFA in Selbstzeugnissen* 308. The student, writing in 1905, describes the "Anneke-student" and writes at the end: "Wir Schülerinnen der Frau Anneke versuchen, bei unsren Kindern anzustreben, was wir von unserer Priesterin empfangen." ("We students of Mrs. Anneke try to pass on to our children the aspirations that we received from our priestess.")

Chapter 9

Conclusion

The almost two decades of Mathilde Anneke's life spent in Milwaukee after the Civil War were dedicated to her work as a teacher, and in terms of her immediate impact, that may well have been her most important work. However, today she is known, if only as a "footnote," for her pioneering work as a journalist (Marzolf 12), and she is also noted as an important early proponent of women's rights, as well as an active member of the Woman Suffrage Movement in the United States (Faust 172–174; Eigler & Kord; and similar reference literature). Her work, like that of so many nineteenth-century German women writers, is marginalized, in her case due in no small part to consideration of her work under the category of German-American-immigrant literature, itself on the margin in comparison to mainstream German literature of the nineteenth century. Her life and work participate in both the negative and positive connotations of marginality with its double bind: "The benefits of other unique perspectives" along with "the disadvantage of being out of the center" (Joeres & Burkhard, *Out of Line/Ausgefallen* 5). Today the literary value of her writing is often seen as less interesting than her social activism. She would have been considered "out of line" in the sense that she did not conform to patriarchal expectations for her gender in her political attitudes, which were, of course, very much "in line" with those of Susan B. Anthony and Elizabeth Cady Stanton. Like other women writers of the nineteenth century, she suffered the penalty for her nonconformity. Although she was a strong woman with firm beliefs about improving the lot of women, at times she would also show sensitivity to ridicule by male liberals, many of whom shared her views in areas outside of the "woman question." However, her literary works, especially those short stories reflecting her sympathy with the Anti-Slavery Movement, demonstrate the positive side of Anneke's perspective from the sidelines in that she strongly identified with the plight of women slaves, and was able to portray their suffering with genuine and effective emotion. While Anneke was certainly well known during her lifetime, especially in the German-American community, assessing her place in history is a difficult task. In this book, I have divided her writings and contributions by chapters, discussing them in the context of the various phases of her life, hoping to provide a balanced view of what she achieved.

In Germany during the period of the Revolution of 1848, she risked ridicule when she published what is arguably her most famous piece of writing, "Das Weib im Conflict mit den socialen Verhältnissen" ("Woman in Conflict with Society"). This early essay, defending Louise Aston and arguing for women's rights in general, was apparently very important to Mathilde Anneke. She published it first as a small booklet in 1847, and then later as excerpts in issue number 2 of her *Frauen-Zeitung*. She reissued it in the United States in her *Deutsche Frauenzeitung*, and again, according to Henkel and Taubert, in the 1860s in the New York *Criminal-Zeitung* (20; also Heinzen 35). The essay must have had special significance to Anneke, or she would hardly have reissued it on four different occasions. It is indeed fortunate that the text was not completely lost, as Henkel thought, and as might well have been the case if we needed to depend on saved copies of these nineteenth-century newspapers. For modern researchers, both a handwritten and typescript copy of the complete essay are available in the Anneke Collection of the Wisconsin Historical Society in Madison, and excerpts are available in Renate Möhrmann's *Frauenemanzipation in deutschen Vormärz: Texte und Dokumente* (82–87). The passion that Anneke brings to her arguments foreshadows the powerful orator she was to become in the support of the Woman Suffrage Movement in the United States. In addition, her affinity for Aston and her respect for her are demonstrated in words of praise for Aston's strength and point of view, and in sympathy for her suffering, as well as in Anneke's willingness to criticize the characterization of Aston's heroine in *Fragment from Her Life*. Anneke showed her own strength of character and independence both in this early work by defending a woman who was the object of a great deal of criticism at the time, as well as in her personal life, by refusing to stay in a marriage of convenience that had turned out badly. Even in her later life, Anneke's students emphasized her integrity as a major reason she was such a role model to them. She, like the Aston she portrays in her essay, refused to be a hypocrite. When she wrote in favor of women's rights, she knew she was risking ridicule, which she also suffered when she accompanied her husband into battle during the Revolution. Her *Memoiren einer Frau aus dem badisch-pfälzischen Feldzüge* (*Memoirs of a Woman from the Baden-Palatinate Campaign*) was written to report her experiences and counteract in part the exaggerated image of what she had taken on.

As a journalist, Anneke entered into traditionally male territory, and as was usual in the nineteenth century she often worked with her husband. In the period of the Revolution of 1848, she carried on the *Neue Kölnische Zeitung* while he was imprisoned (his co-editor provided funding but was not actively involved), and when the newspaper was banned, she immediately got around the ban by starting her own *Frauen-Zeitung* with the same revolutionary tone and activist nature. Thus it is apparent that while she worked with her husband as part of a common cause during the Revolution, she was fully capable of carrying on the work by herself. Once Fritz and Mathilde Anneke immigrated to the United States, Mathilde planned to continue her newspaper. Like other nineteenth-century women publishers in the United States who are remembered today, Anneke was an outspoken crusader for women's rights, abolition, and social justice. Her "sharp and biting style" certainly fit in with the times, although other well-known publishers such as Victoria Woodhull and Annie Royall were still frequently labeled "social oddities" (Marzolf 11). Anneke's work may have been more acceptable to the German Forty-Eighters since her revolutionary activities in Germany had already won her recognition. When she established her *Deutsche Frauenzeitung* in Milwaukee in 1852, in line with her belief that women should be able to do whatever professional work they were qualified to do, she wanted to employ women typesetters. However, the constraints against women in skilled professions were not always the result of a lack of knowledge or training. Just as there was opposition to women entering fields such as medicine or law, well-paid blue-collar jobs could also be closed to women by men fearing the impact on their own jobs. When Anneke tried to hire women typesetters, the all-male unions vehemently opposed her and refused to let women join the union.

Anneke's experience with the male typesetters' union did not diminish her appreciation of what education could do to improve the lot of women. While she knew that education alone could not open all the doors professionally for women, she was acutely aware that without the appropriate education or training, women could not hope to compete. When she planned her school in Milwaukee, her curriculum was based on that of male institutions so that her female students would be prepared to take on the responsibilities their talents allowed as society changed in its acceptance of women on an equal basis with men. During her lifetime, the number of women teachers increased dramatically, and some of her own students were preparing for a career in teaching with Anneke as their role model. Although she did not found her school until the last part of her life, she considered educational issues, especially the education of young children, in her early newspaper writing in Germany. In addition, as was the case of many nineteenth-century women, she was acutely aware of the weaknesses of her own education, and she regretted her own lack of knowledge and accomplishment especially in the area of languages. Still, she enjoyed learning and read extensively in order to prepare her later classes and lectures on German literature, and she was also well informed on the major social issues of her time.

If the argument in favor of basic literacy for women often revolves around the idea of social control—consider the number of "conduct books" for women during the period 1830–1860[1]—it must be remembered that women's attitudes developed on an individual basis as well. The ideal images of women, such as "Republican Motherhood" and "True Womanhood," were certainly quite prevalent and served to foster an accepted image of what a woman should be. At the same time, many women writers emerged during the nineteenth century, very often as a means for women to earn a living at a time when few other professional avenues were open to them. Journalism and publishing allowed such women as Mathilde Anneke to write in their own voice, and made radical ideas available to other women as well. Thus, the metaphor of the "double-edge sword" applies to literacy, in that it "can be used for social control" while at the same time it "also has the tendency to become private and idiosyncratic, veering off in unexpected and unsettling directions" (Hobbs 10). Once the majority of women became literate, they became exposed to both radical and conservative ideas, and then could use their skills, including the opportunity to lecture in public, to contribute to the public debate. Mathilde Anneke's radical ideas were very accessible to the German-American community both through her writing and through her public lectures on social issues.

Anneke used her writing skills, especially during the Civil War, to support the Anti-Slavery forces. Her most famous stories in support of abolition were "Gebrochene Ketten" ("Broken Chains"), which appeared in 1864 in the *Milwaukee Herald* and *Der Bund*, and "Die Sclaven-Auction" ("The Slave Auction"), which appeared in 1862 in *Didaskalia*. In addition she wrote newspaper articles in Europe, reporting on the progress of the Civil War, and on the views and actions of major political figures. Fritz Anneke was fighting, meanwhile, on the Union side, and Mathilde Anneke's viewpoint would have been quite evident in her reporting.

However, her greatest political activism and contributions were in the area of women's rights. From the moment she arrived in the United States, she connected with strong women and formed lasting friendships with them. Included among them was Ernestine L. Rose, whom Anneke admired for her radical thinking and strength of her convictions ("Radikalismus ihres Denkens und die Entschiedenheit ihres Auftretens in jeder Richtung"), and for her willingness to identify as enemies religion, the papacy, and the Bible (*MFA in Selbstzeugnissen* 321). Anneke was of like mind in openly confronting religious hypocrisy, and she never wavered in this aspect of her thinking, which she often incorporated in her speeches. Another question where she remained firm throughout her life was her view of suffrage and temperance as separate issues. As Bus writes in her article, "Mathilde Anneke and the Suffrage Movement" (83), Anneke "reminded both her American and her German audiences that temperance had no bearing whatsoever on the issue of women's rights and that equity for women was demanded by justice and reason." On this question, she was very much in tune with the German-American community, which she believed could be persuaded to support suffrage, but which, she knew, strongly opposed the temperance movement.

She was an early admirer of Susan B. Anthony and Elizabeth Cady Stanton, and the major part of her activities in support of woman suffrage occurred in the period before the Civil War and her return to Europe. When she returned to the United States after the Civil War, her work was focused mainly on her school, and her activities in support of women's rights became more concentrated on the state level. However, her connection with major movement leaders did not wane. In March 1869 when Susan B. Anthony and Elizabeth Cady Stanton arrived in Milwaukee on a lecture tour, Anneke spoke at the opening of the conference (Roethke 46). Then in May 1869, Anneke, in her role as association vice president for the state of Wisconsin, attended the conference of the Equal Rights Association in New York and spoke to the assembly, where she focused on women's "thirst for scientific knowledge—that fountain of all peacefully progressing amelioration in human history" (Roethke 47 cites *History of Woman Suffrage* 392–394). She spoke of the importance of reason and lamented that: "This longing [for scientific knowledge], this effort of reason seeking knowledge of itself, of ideas, conclusions, and all higher things, has, as far as historical remembrance goes back, never been so violently suppressed in any human being as in women" (Roethke 47). Anneke demonstrated in this speech that her rhetorical power and passion remained intact at this stage of her life, and that she felt very strongly about the progress that she believed education could bring to women's lives. Her work with the school was thus united with her work for women's rights. When the Equal Rights Association split over the question of support for the Fifteenth Amendment, Anneke, as we have seen, supported Anthony and Stanton and stayed with the new National Woman Suffrage Association, serving as vice president. She lobbied in Washington in 1870 for women's right to vote and was an effective speaker for that cause. Her later speeches, such as her 1872 speech for the dedication of the German Hall in Milwaukee[2] and her 1873 speech on the conviction of Susan B. Anthony,[3] show her continued involvement in the Suffrage Movement, as long as her health permitted. The correspondence between Anneke and Suffrage leaders show how highly she was valued, both personally and for her efforts on behalf on the organization. In 1876 when she injured her hand, which never healed properly and left her disabled, both Susan B. Anthony (August 1876) and Elizabeth Cady Stanton (October 1876) wrote of their concern in their personal letters to her (*MFA in Selbstzeugnissen* 301–302). In 1880 Anneke delivered the address of welcome at the NWSA conference in Milwaukee (Heinzen 207), but at that point she no longer traveled to national conventions outside of the city.

As a nineteenth-century rebel, Mathilde Franziska Anneke did not accept traditional society's definition of what she should be. She, Anthony, and Stanton were very likeminded individuals. Anneke would have agreed with Stanton's observations on womanliness at the National American Woman Suffrage Association conference of 1890, since she was willing to risk even the pain of ridicule to define herself. Like other women who were considered radical in their time, she chafed at the male idea of "womanliness": "to have a manner which pleases him—quiet, deferential, submissive, approaching him as a subject does a master" (Schneir 155). Stanton reminded her listeners at the 1890 conference, which reunited the two factions of the U.S. woman's movement, and took place just a few years after Anneke's death, that society did not yet know what real womanliness might be. In her words: "Man has spoken in the State, the Church and the Home, and made the codes, creeds and customs which govern every relation in life, and women have simply echoed all his thoughts and walked in the paths he prescribed" (Schneir 156).

Her call was to leave behind the virtues of patience and persuasiveness used when dealing with children, and to compel people of reason who understand justice to realize the justice of granting full rights to women, who, like men, have the "gift of reason" and the duty to act in the name of truth.

Throughout her life, Mathilde Anneke did exactly that. As new scholarship rediscovers her contributions—to journalism on both sides of the Atlantic, to the German Revolution of 1848, to German exile literature, to the Woman Suffrage Movement as an early contributor to feminist thought weighing in on the *Frauenfrage*, and to the education of young women in Milwaukee—the value of her activist life and writings will become an integral and better known part of nineteenth-century history.

NOTES

1. Hobbs, especially Jane E. Rose's article, "Conduct Books for Women, 1830–1860: A Rationale for Women's Conduct and Domestic Role in America," 37–58.
2. The full text of this speech, which I have translated into English, appears in Chapter 6 of this book.
3. My translation of the text appears in Chapter 6.

Bibliography

Works by Mathilde Franziska Giesler Anneke

Des Christen freudigen Aufblick zum himmlischen Vater (*A Christian's Joyful Look Upward to the Heavenly Father*), 1839.

Das Geisterhaus in New York (*The Haunted House in New York*). Jena & Leipzig: Costenoble, 1864. (Translation of an incomplete anonymous serial novel; Anneke is the author of the final chapter.)

"Gebrochene Ketten" ("Broken Chains"). *Milwaukee Herald*, June 1864; *Der Bund*, June 1864. Wisconsin Historical Society, Madison, has a copy of this work in its archives. (See Chapter 7, footnote 2 of this book.) The text is also available in: *Die gebrochenen Ketten: Erzählungen, Reportagen und Reden (1861–1873)*. Maria Wagner, ed. Stuttgart: Hans-Dieter Akademischer Verlag, 1983, 9–25.

Die gebrochenen Ketten: Erzählungen, Reportagen und Reden (1861–1873) (*Broken Chains: Stories, Reports, and Speeches*). Hrsg. und mit Nachwort versehen von Maria Wagner. Stuttgart: Hans-Dieter Heinz Akademischer Verlag, 1983.

Der Meister ist da und rufet Dich (*The Lord Is Here and Calls You*), 1841.

Memoiren einer Frau aus dem badisch-pfälzischen Feldzüge (*Memoirs of a Woman from the Baden-Palatinate Campaign*). Newark, NJ, 1853. Reprinted in: Henkel and Taubert, *Das Weib im Conflict mit den socialen Verhältnissen: Mathilde Franziska Anneke und die erste deutsche Frauenzeitung*. Bochum, 1976, 63–121.

Oithono, oder die Tempelweihe. Wesel, 1842.

"Die Sclaven-Auction" ("The Slave Auction"). *Didaskalia*, June 1862. Available in: Maria Wagner, ed., *Die gebrochenen Ketten: Erzählungen, Reportagen und Reden (1861–1873)*. Stuttgart: Hans-Dieter Akademischer Verlag, 1983, 27–47.

"Uhland in Texas." *Illinois Staatszeitung*, April 1866. Available in: Maria Wagner, ed., *Die gebrochenen Ketten: Erzählungen, Reportagen und Reden (1861–1873)*. Stuttgart: Hans-Dieter Akademischer Verlag, 1983, 49–190.

"Das Weib im Conflict mit den socialen Verhältnissen" ("Woman in Conflict with Society"). *Neue Kölnische Zeitung*, 1847. Abridged text in German available in: Renate Möhrmann, ed., *Frauenemanzipation im deutschen Vormärz: Texte und Dokumente*. Stuttgart: Reclam, 1978, 82–87.

Das Weib im Conflict mit den socialen Verhältnissen, ts [orig. ms. M97-253]. Fritz Anneke & Mathilde Franziska Anneke Collection. WisMssLW Box 6 Folder 7. Wisconsin Historical Society, Madison, 1847.

Works Edited by Mathilde Franziska Giesler Anneke

These books also include work written by her: poetry, short stories, a travelogue, essays, and translations.

Damenalmanach (Almanac for Ladies), 1841.

Heimatgruß (Greetings from the Homeland), 1840.

Westfälisches Jahrbuch: Produkte der Rothen Erde (Westphalian Yearbook: Products of the Red Earth), 1846.

Newspapers Published by Anneke

Die Frauen-Zeitung. First issue: September 27, 1848.

Die Deutsche Frauen-Zeitung. First issue: March 1, 1852.

Primary Sources by 19th-Century Authors

Anthony, Susan B., and Ida Husted Harper, eds. *The History of Woman Suffrage: 1883–1900.* Vol. 4. Rochester: Susan B. Anthony, 1902.

Aston, Louise. *Meine Emancipation, Verweisung und Rechtfertigung. (My Emancipation, Exile, and Defense).* Brussels, 1846. Text of "Die Verweisung" also available in: *Emanzipation im deutschen Vormärz: Texte und Dokumente*, Renate Möhrmann, ed., Stuttgart: Reclam, 1978, 68–82.

Beecher, Catharine E. *Woman's Profession as Mother and Educator, with Views in Opposition to Woman Suffrage.* Philadelphia and Boston: George Maclean, 1872.

Blackwell, Jeannine, and Susanne Zantop, eds. *Bitter Healing: German Women Writers from 1700–1830. An Anthology.* Lincoln & London: University of Nebraska Press, 1990.

Büchner, Luise. "Eine Reise-Erinnerung" (1875; "A Travel Memoir"). *"Gebildet, ohne gelehrt zu sein": Essays, Berichte und Briefe von Luise Büchner zur Geschichte ihrer Zeit.* Margarete Dierks, ed. Darmstadt: Justus von Liebig Verlag, 1991, 221–236.

———. *Über weibliche Berufsarten. (On the Types of Occupations for Women)* Hrsg. v. Mentor. Darmstadt: C. Köhler, [1872]. (Microfiche. Glen Park, NJ: Microfilming Corp. of America, 1975. *The Gerritsen Collection of Women's History*, No. 408.)

———. *Women and Their Vocation: A Nineteenth-Century View. [Die Frauen und ihr Beruf].* Trans. and with an Introduction by Susan L. Piepke. New York: Peter Lang, 1999. (Vol. 5: *Women in German Literature*, Peter D.G. Brown, ed.).

Dierks, Margarete, ed. *"Gebildet, ohne gelehrt zu sein": Essays, Berichte und Briefe von Luise Büchner zur Geschichte ihrer Zeit. ("Educated, without being learned": Essays, Reports, and Letters on the History of Her Times by Luise Büchner)* Darmstadt: Justus von Liebig Verlag, 1991.

Ebner-Eschenbach, Marie von. *Seven Stories by Marie von Ebner-Eschenbach.* Trans. and with an Introduction by Helga H. Harriman. Columbia, SC: Camden House, Inc., 1986.

Hahn-Hahn, Ida Gräfin. *Orientalische Briefe.* 3 vols. Berlin: Verlag von Alexander Duncker, 1844.

Lewald, Fanny. *The Education of Fanny Lewald: An Autobiography.* Trans. Hanna Ballin Lewis. Albany: State University of New York Press, 1992.

———. *Politische Schriften für und wider die Frauen.* Hrsg. Ulrike Helmer. Frankfurt: Ulrike Helmer Verlag, 1989.

Möhrmann, Renate, ed. *Frauenemanzipation im deutschen Vormärz: Texte und Dokumente.* (*Women's Emancipation in the German Vormärz: Texts and Documents*) Stuttgart: Reclam, 1978.

National Woman Suffrage Association. *The Report of the International Council of Women.* March 25–April 1, 1888. Susan B. Anthony Collection in the Library of Congress, Washington, DC.

Stanton, Elizabeth Cady, Susan B. Anthony, and Matilda Joslyn Gage. *The History of Woman Suffrage: 1848–1861.* Vol. 1. New York: Arno and the *New York Times,* 1969.

Varnhagen, Rahel Levin. *Rahel: Ein Buch des Andenkens für ihre Freunde.* Berlin, 1834.

Wagner, Maria. *Mathilde Franziska Anneke in Selbstzeugnissen und Dokumenten.* (*Mathilde Franziska Anneke in Her Own Testimony and Documents*) Frankfurt am Main: Fischer, 1980.

Was die Deutschen aus Amerika berichteten, 1828–1865. (*What Germans Reported from America, 1828–1865*) Hrsg. und mit einem Nachwort von Maria Wagner. Stuttgart: Hans-Dieter Heinz Akademischer Verlag, 1985.

Secondary Sources

Anderson, Bonnie S., and Judith P. Zinsser. *A History of Their Own: Women in Europe from Prehistory to the Present.* Vol. 2. New York: Harper & Row, 1988.

Alexander, Thomas. *The Prussian Elementary Schools.* New York: Macmillan Company, 1919.

Blackwell, Hildegard Wallner. "Mathilde Franziska Anneke: An Early Feminist (1817–1884)." *Society for German American Studies Newsletter* 16.1 (1995): 2–4.

Blos, Anna. *Frauen der deutschen Revolution 1848.* Dresden, 1928.

Brancaforte, Charlotte L., ed. *The German Forty-Eighters in the United States.* New York: Peter Lang, 1989.

Brinker-Gabler, Gisela, ed. *Encountering the Other(s): Studies in Literature, History, and Culture.* Albany: SUNY Press, 1995.

Bus, Annette P. "Mathilde Anneke and the Suffrage Movement." *The German Forty-Eighters in the United States.* Charlotte L. Brancaforte, ed. New York: Peter Lang, 1989, 79–92.

Cott, Nancy F. *The Grounding of Modern Feminism.* New Haven and London: Yale University Press, 1987.

Daley, Margaretmary. *Women of Letters: A Study of Self and Genre in the Personal Writing of Caroline Schlegel-Schelling, Rahel Levin Varnhagen, and Bettina von Arnim.* Columbia, SC: Camden House, 1998.

Diethe, Carol. *Towards Emancipation: German Women Writers of the Nineteenth Century.* New York, Oxford: Berghahn, 1998.

DuBois, Ellen Carol. *Feminism and Suffrage: The Emergence of an Independent Women's Movement in America 1848–1869.* Ithaca and London: Cornell University Press, 1978.

Eigler, Friederike, and Susanne Kord, eds. *The Feminist Encyclopedia of German Literature.* Westport, CT: Greenwood Press, 1997.

Evans, Richard J. *The Feminists: Women's Emancipation Movements in Europe, America and Australasia 1840–1920.* New York: Barnes & Noble, 1977.

Faust, Albert B. "Mathilde Franziska Giesler-Anneke." *German American Literature.* Metuchen, NJ, and London: Scarecrow Press, 1977, 172–178.

Flexner, Eleanor. *Century of Struggle: The Woman's Rights Movement in the United States.* New York: Atheneum, 1974.

Fout, John, ed. *German Women in the Nineteenth Century: A Social History.* New York and London: Holmes & Meier, 1984.

French, Lorely. *German Women as Letter Writers: 1750–1850.* Madison: Fairleigh Dickinson Press, 1996.

Frevert, Ute. *Women in German History: From Bourgeois Emancipation to Sexual Liberation.* [*Frauen-Geschichte zwischen bürgerlicher Verbesserung und neuer Weiblichkeit*]. Trans. Stuart McKinnon-Evans with Barbara Norden and Terry Bond. Oxford and Washington, DC, 1988, reprint 1995.

Frost, Elizabeth, and Kathryn Cullen-DuPont. *Women's Suffrage in America: An Eyewitness History.* New York and Oxford: Facts On File, 1992.

Gebhardt, Manfred. *Mathilde Franziska Anneke, Madame, Soldat und Suffragette: Biografie.* Berlin: Verlag Neues Leben, 1988.

Gerhard, Ute. "Über die Anfänge der deutschen Frauenbewegung um 1848." ("On the Beginnings of the German Women's Movement Around 1848") *Frauen suchen ihre Geschichte. Historische Studien zum 19. Und 20. Jarhundert.* Hrsg. Karen Hausen. München: C.H. Beck, 1983, 196–220.

Giele, Janet Zollinger. *Two Paths to Women's Equality: Temperance, Suffrage, and the Origins of Modern Feminism.* New York: Twayne Publishers, 1995.

Goldberg, Bettina. "The Forty-Eighters in America: The Theory and Practice of Reform." *The German Forty-Eighters in the United States.* Charlotte L. Brancaforte, ed. New York: Peter Lang, 1989, 203–208.

Goodman, Kay. "The Impact of Rahel Varnhagen on Women in the 19th Century." *Amsterdamer Beiträge* 10 (1980): 125–153.

Heinzen, Henrietta M. *Biographical Notes.* Typed manuscript. Fritz Anneke and Mathilde Franziska Anneke Collection, Wisconsin Historical Society, Madison.

Henkel, Martin, and Rolf Taubert. *Das Weib im Conflict mit den socialen Verhältnissen. Mathilde Franziska Anneke und die erste deutsche Frauenzeitung. (Woman in Con-*

flict with Society. Mathilde Franziska Anneke and the First German Women's Newspaper) Bochum: Verlag edition égalité, 1976.

Hense-Jensen, Wilhelm. *Wisconsin's Deutsch-Amerikaner bis zum Schluß des neunzehnten Jahrhunderts*. 1. Band. Milwaukee: Verlag der Deutschen Gesellschaft, 1900.

Hippel, Theodor Gottlieb von. *Über die bürgerliche Verbesserung der Weiber* (*On the Civil Improvement of Women*), 1792.

Hobbs, Catherine, ed., intro. *Nineteenth-Century Women Learn to Write*. Charlottesville and London: University Press of Virginia, 1995.

Isenberg, Nancy. *Sex and Citizenship in Antebellum America*. Chapel Hill and London: North Carolina Press, 1998.

Joeres, Ruth-Ellen Boetcher. "1848 from a Distance: German Women Writers on the Revolution." *Modern Language Notes* 97:3 (April 1982), 590–614.

———. *Respectability and Deviance: Nineteenth-Century German Women Writers and the Ambiguity of Representation*. Chicago and London: University of Chicago Press, 1998.

Joeres, Ruth-Ellen Boetcher, and Marianne Burkhard, eds. *Out of Line/Ausgefallen: The Paradox of Marginality in the Writings of Nineteeth-Century German Women*. Amsterdam: Rodopi, 1989 (Bd. 28: *Amsterdamer Beiträge zur neueren Germanistik*).

Joeres, Ruth-Ellen Boetcher, and Mary Jo Maynes, eds. *German Women in the Eighteenth and Nineteenth Centuries: A Social and Literary History*. Bloomington: Indiana University Press, 1986.

Kaarsberg Wallach, Martha. "Women of German-American Fiction: Therese Robinson, Mathilde Anneke, and Fernande Richter." *America and the Germans: An Assessment of a Three-Hundred-Year History. I: Immigration, Language, Ethnicity*. Frank Trommler and Joseph McVeigh, eds. Philadelphia: University of Pennsylvania Press, 1985, 331–342.

Kleinberg, S. J. *Women in the United States 1830–1945*. New Brunswick, NJ: Rutgers University Press, 1999.

Krueger, Lillian. "Madame Mathilda Franziska Anneke: An Early Wisconsin Journalist." *Wisconsin Magazine of History*. December 1937, 160–167.

Lerner, Gerda. *The Creation of Feminist Consciousness: From the Middle Ages to Eighteen-Seventy*. New York and Oxford: Oxford University Press, 1993.

———. *The Majority Finds Its Past: Placing Women in History*. Oxford: Oxford University Press, 1979.

Lumsden, Linda J. *Rampant Women: Suffragists and the Right of Assembly*. Knoxville: The University of Tennessee Press, 1997.

Marzolf, Marion. *Up From the Footnote: A History of Women Journalists*. New York: Hastings House, 1977.

Möhrmann, Renate. *Die andere Frau: Emanzipationsansätze deutscher Schriftstellerinnen im Vorfeld der Achtundvierziger Revolution*. (*The Other Woman: Starting Points for the Emancipation of German Women Writers Immediately Prior to the Revolution of 1848*) Stuttgart: Metzler, 1977.

Ohnesorg, Stephanie. *Mit Kompaß, Kutsche und Kamel. (Rück-) Einbindung der Frau in die Geschichte des Reisens und Reiseliteratur*. (*With Compass, Carriage, and Camel*.

(Re-) Connecting Woman to the History of Travel and Travel Literature) St. Ingbert: Röhrig Universitätsverlag, 1996.

Poore, Carol J. *German-American Socialist Literature 1865–1900.* Bern and Frankfurt am Main: Peter Lang, 1982.

Rippley, La Vern J. *The German-Americans.* Boston: Twayne Publishers, 1976.

Robertson, Priscilla. *An Experience of Women: Pattern and Change in Nineteenth-Century Europe.* Philadelphia: Temple University Press, 1982.

Roethke, Gisela. "M.F. Anneke: Eine Vormärzkämpferin für Frauenrechte in Deutschland und in den Vereinigten Staaten." ("M. F. Anneke: A Fighter in the *Vormärz* Period for Women's Rights in Germany and in the United States") *Yearbook of German-American Studies.* 28 (1993): 33–51.

Ruben, Regina. *Mathilde Franziska Anneke, die erste große deutsche Verfechterin des Frauenstimmrechts.* (*Mathilde Franziska Anneke, the First Great German Champion for Women's Right to Vote*) Hamburg: Verlag R. Ruben, 1906.

Rury, John L. *Education and Women's Work: Female Schooling and the Division of Labor in Urban America, 1870–1930.* Albany: SUNY Press, 1991.

Schneir, Miriam, ed., intro. *Feminism: The Essential Historical Writings.* New York: Vintage, 1994.

Schulte, Wilhelm. *Westfälische Lebensbilder.* Nr. 8: *Mathilde Franziska Anneke.* Münster, 1958.

Sheehan, James J. *German History 1770–1866.* Oxford: Clarendon Press, 1989.

Solomon, Barbara Miller. *In the Company of Educated Women: A History of Women and Higher Education in America.* New Haven and London: Yale University Press, 1985.

Stuecher, Dorothea Diver. *Twice Removed: The Experience of German-American Women Writers in the 19th Century.* New York: Peter Lang, 1990.

Thompson, Eleanor Wolf. *Education for Ladies 1830–1860: Ideas on Education in Magazines for Women.* Morningside Heights, NY: King's Crown Press, 1947.

Tolzmann, Don Heinrich. *German American Literature.* Metuchen, NJ, and London: Scarecrow Press, 1977.

Twellmann, Margrit. *Die Deutsche Frauenbewegung im Spiegel repräsentativer Frauenzeitschriften. Ihre Anfänge und erste Entwicklung 1843–1889.* (*The German Women's Movement Mirrored in Representative Women's Magazines. Their Beginnings and Early Development 1843–1889*) Meisenheim am Glan: Verlag Anton Hain, 1972.

Wagner, Maria. "Feminismus, Literatur und Revolution—ein unveröffentliches Manuskript aus dem Jahre 1850." ("Feminism, Literature, and Revolution—An Unpublished Manuscript from the Year 1850") *The German Quarterly* 50.2 (1977): 121–129.

———. "A German Writer and Feminist in 19th-Century America." *Beyond the Eternal Feminine: Critical Essays on Women and German Literature.* Susan L. Cocalis and Kay Goodman, eds. Stuttgart: Hans-Dieter Heinz Akademischer Verlag, 1982, 159–172.

———. "Mathilde Anneke's Stories of Slavery in the German-American Press." *MELUS* 6.2 (Winter 1979): 9–16.

Wheeler, Marjorie Spruill, ed. *One Woman, One Vote: Rediscovering the Woman Suffrage Movement.* Troutdale, Oregon: New Sage Press, 1995.

Wittke, Carl Frederich. *Refugees of Revolution: The German Forty-Eighters in America.* Philadelphia: University of Pennsylvania Press, 1952.

Woody, Thomas. *A History of Women's Education in the United States.* Vol. 1. New York: Octagon Books, Inc., 1966.

Index